Welcome

Whether you're barbecuing for friends in the sunshine, sitting round the table with family on a snowy Christmas day or simply rustling up some grub for yourself on a rainy evening, one thing remains constant - good food is good food no matter what time of year. We've put together a collection of recipes for every season. We've got you covered for the holidays and celebrations with Easter and Christmas feasts, as well as Halloween, Bonfire, Valentine's and Pancake Day treats. Plus, enjoy experimenting with fresh ingredients in the spring, dining al fresco and picnic ideas for the summer, comfort food and warming puds for the autumn and plenty of party food to keep you smiling on those cold winter evenings. Finally, make the most of food at every time of year with our seasonal guides on what to eat and how to use available produce. Start your year-long journey of delicious recipes today. Let's get cooking!

CONTENTS

SPRING

08 What's in season?
Spotlight on asparagus
As the days start to get warmer and plants start to bloom, there's a wealth of fresh ingredients to enjoy during spring

12 A taste of spring
Easy ways to make fresh and tasty seasonal ingredients the star of your meal

20 Serve up an Easter feast
Delicious recipes to impress your guests

28 Easter sweet treats
Delight friends and family with one of these creations

SUMMER

40 What's in season?
Spotlight on strawberries
There's no better time for fresh produce than in summer; it's a great time to tuck in to fruit and veg, as well as seafood

44 A taste of summer
Bring a dose of sunshine to your kitchen with these mouthwatering recipes

52 Fire up the bbq
Whether your guests are vegetarian, pescatarian or meat lovers, there's something for everyone in this al fresco recipe collection

66 Simply sweet treats
Easy and refreshing desserts that'll let you maximise your time in the sun

76 Pack a picnic
Fill your basket with these tempting treats and head out into the great outdoors

11 Asparagus and pea carbonara

57 Thai spiced turkey burgers with Asian slaw

88 Pesto roasted squash

Halloumi, carrot and bean tacos 18

4 woman&home SEASONAL COOKBOOK

72 Raspberry Mousse

Sausage and butternut squash stew **99**

AUTUMN

86 What's in season?
Spotlight on pumpkin
Autumn sees the arrival of comforting root vegetables

90 Feeding a crowd
Autumnal warmers to guarantee stress-free entertaining

104 Warming puds
Celebrate seasonal fruits with these delicious, autumnal puds

114 Halloween treats
These recipes for the spookiest night of the year are scarily good

116 Firework feasts
Tasty autumn warmers perfect for a bonfire night gathering

WINTER

120 What's in season?
Spotlight on pomegranate
Winter is a great time of year to find colourful produce to brighten up your festive feasts

124 A Christmas feast
Stay on track for the best festive lunch ever with our simple countdown

138 Something sweet
Indulgent treats for the holiday season

148 Our kind of party
Open the bubbly and get the soirée started with these easy-to-make nibbles

158 My sweet Valentine
Why not make one of these irresistible bakes for your loved one?

160 Perfect pancakes
Flipping great recipes for Pancake Day

Meringue stack pavlova **34**

SEASONAL COOKBOOK woman&home 5

Spring

10	**Asparagus prosciutto and burrata toasts**
10	**Nutty asparagus quinoa**
11	**Asparagus and pea carbonara**
11	**Asparagus and kale shakshuka**
13	**Gnocchi with ricotta and cauliflower**
14	**All-in-one lamb roast**
14	**Baked vanilla cheesecake with candied rhubarb**
15	**Asparagus eggs Benedict**
16	**Pink grapefruit, black bean and rice salad**
18	**Cod with miso butter**
18	**Halloumi, carrot and bean tacos**
19	**Apple and blueberry cobbler**
22	**Crispy asparagus with maple syrup**
22	**Courgette tart with feta**
24	**Minted pea soup**
25	**Lamb en croûte with basil and mint stuffing**
25	**Golden potato gratin**
26	**Spiced aubergine and courgette tabbouleh**
26	**Lemon cheesecake tart**
30	**Triple-decker simnel cake**
31	**Easter egg rocky road**
32	**Chocolate babka**
33	**Easter bunny melting moments**
33	**Spiced chocolate cupcakes**
34	**Meringue stack pavlova**
35	**Lavender and vanilla custard pudding**
36	**Hot cross bun bombes**
37	**Cinnamon and apple hot cross bun wreath**

SPRING

What's in SEASON

As the days start to get warmer and plants start to bloom, there's a wealth of fresh ingredients to enjoy during the spring

✣ CRAB
The best crabmeat is 'hand-picked', so choose British pot-caught crab for the most sustainable option. Crab has a subtle flavour so make it the star of the show – a traditional dressed crab is a quick and easy starter that will delight your guests.

✣ JERSEY ROYALS
The boys are back in town. This little and nutty-flavoured new potato variety is grown exclusively on the island of Jersey, where the climate is optimal. Lovely simply boiled, leave the skins on for flavour, serve warm with butter and chopped chives or cold in salads.

✣ MINT
A fantastic flavour-enhancing herb, make a mint sauce to serve with lamb, add to a chocolate for an after-dinner delight or serve with peas for a flavour match made in heaven. If you have leftovers, simply steep in boiled water with a spoonful of honey for a refreshing fresh mint tea.

✣ PASSION FRUIT
For an easy way to jazz up a bowl of yoghurt or fruit salad drizzle over the zingy pulp of a passion fruit. Grown in hot climates such as those of Colombia and the Caribbean, you will find mostly the dark purple 'edulis' variety imported to the UK.

A few torn mint leaves tossed with any other salad leaves adds an extra fresh-tasting note to your side dish or salad main.

✣ PLAICE
Your plaice or mine? This versatile flatfish with a delicate flavour swims back into season from spring until early autumn. Choose plaice caught in the North Sea or eastern English Channel, where there are sufficient sustainable stocks. It's perfect pan fried with a lemon and parsley butter.

✣ RADISHES
A much-loved vegetable in our Test Kitchen, we love them chopped in salads, pickled, or even roasted. Versatile radishes are bursting with vitamins A, B6, C, E, and K plus a range of minerals. They are also high in antioxidants and packed full of fibre and flavour.

✣ RHUBARB
Forced rhubarb (the fluorescent pink variety from the nine square mile 'triangle' in West Yorkshire where it's grown in the dark and picked by candlelight) sadly comes to an end at the end of March. But thankfully the regular variety emerges from the soil ready for harvest in April. Here's a nifty trick: we always add a little grenadine or beetroot juice when we cook rhubarb to enhance the vibrant colour.

✣ SPRING LAMB
British lamb comes back on the menu just in time for Easter lunch. Spring lamb is extremely tender and as it's young it also has a more delicate taste than lamb bought later in the year, so ideal for those that don't like a strong flavour. Flick through to see our recipe for a lovely lamb en croûte with basil and mint stuffing.

✣ SORREL
With a sharp sour flavour that tastes a little lemony, sorrel is a unique leaf. Hugh Fearnley-Whittingstall describes it as tasting of spring. It's easy to grow but harder to come by in supermarkets. If you can get your hands on it use it sparingly, peppering it through your dishes. In Greece it's sometimes used in spanakopita and in Poland added to soup.

✣ SPINACH
Sorrel's distant cousin spinach is back too in spring. As Popeye probably taught you, it's very good for you, it's certainly full of iron and it's also one of the most versatile leaves.

✣ WILD GARLIC
Forget the chocolate eggs, head out foraging on your own hunt for delicious wild garlic. With a distinct smell, you should be able to sniff it out in deciduous woodlands and along riverbanks. You can use both the leaves and flowers to flavour dishes. Make wild garlic pesto by blitzing Parmesan, pine nuts, olive oil and a squeeze of lemon.

WHAT'S IN SEASON

Just 150g of asparagus provides 200mcg of folic acid, the recommended daily intake for most adults.

ASPARAGUS
✣ Is there a vegetable more synonymous with spring? Asparagus has a short season and is at it's very best in April, so it makes the perfect side for your Easter feast. Enjoy our selection of quick and simple dishes to make the most of these fabulous spears.

Asparagus, prosciutto and burrata toasts

TIP Buffalo mozzarella is a good alternative to burrata.

Nutty asparagus quinoa

Full of goodness, this makes the perfect filling salad

Serves 4 • Ready in 15 mins

For the dressing:
1 shallot, finely chopped
1 chilli, finely chopped
1tsp sesame oil
125ml (4fl oz) olive oil
Juice and zest of 1 lemon
1 bunch basil, torn
1 bunch mint, chopped

For the salad:
100g (3½oz) baby spinach leaves
2 x 250g (9oz) pouches Merchant Gourmet ready-cooked quinoa
100g (3½oz) mixed cashew nuts and macadamias, toasted
400g (14oz) asparagus spears, blanched
2tbsp sunflower seeds

1 Mix together all the ingredients for the salad dressing.
2 In a separate, large bowl, toss together the spinach leaves, quinoa, nuts and asparagus spears. Stir through the dressing, scatter with sunflower seeds and serve.
Per serving: Cals 690, Fat 48g, Sat fat 7.5g, Carbs 43g

TIP Using a precooked microwavable pack of quinoa makes this dish super speedy.

Asparagus, prosciutto and burrata toasts

A classy twist on the ham toasty, we love this for a speedy supper

Serves 4 • Ready in 10 mins

1tbsp mustard powder
1tsp soft brown sugar
4tbsp single cream
200g (7oz) asparagus, halved lengthways
4 thick slices good-quality sourdough
butter, for toast
2 balls burrata cheese
100g (3½oz) prosciutto slices
Extra virgin olive oil, to serve
2tbsp sesame seeds, to serve

1 Mix the mustard powder, sugar and cream together with 2tbsp water. Set aside to thicken while you prepare the sourdough toasts.
2 Heat a griddle pan and griddle the asparagus for 2 mins each side until cooked through and slightly charred.
3 Toast and butter the sourdough. Spread with the mustard cream and top with the burrata, asparagus and prosciutto. Drizzle with olive oil and sprinkle with sesame seeds to serve.
Per serving: Cals 513, Fat 32g, Sat fat 17g, Carbs 27g

Nutty asparagus quinoa

GREAT FOR VEGANS
GLUTEN FREE

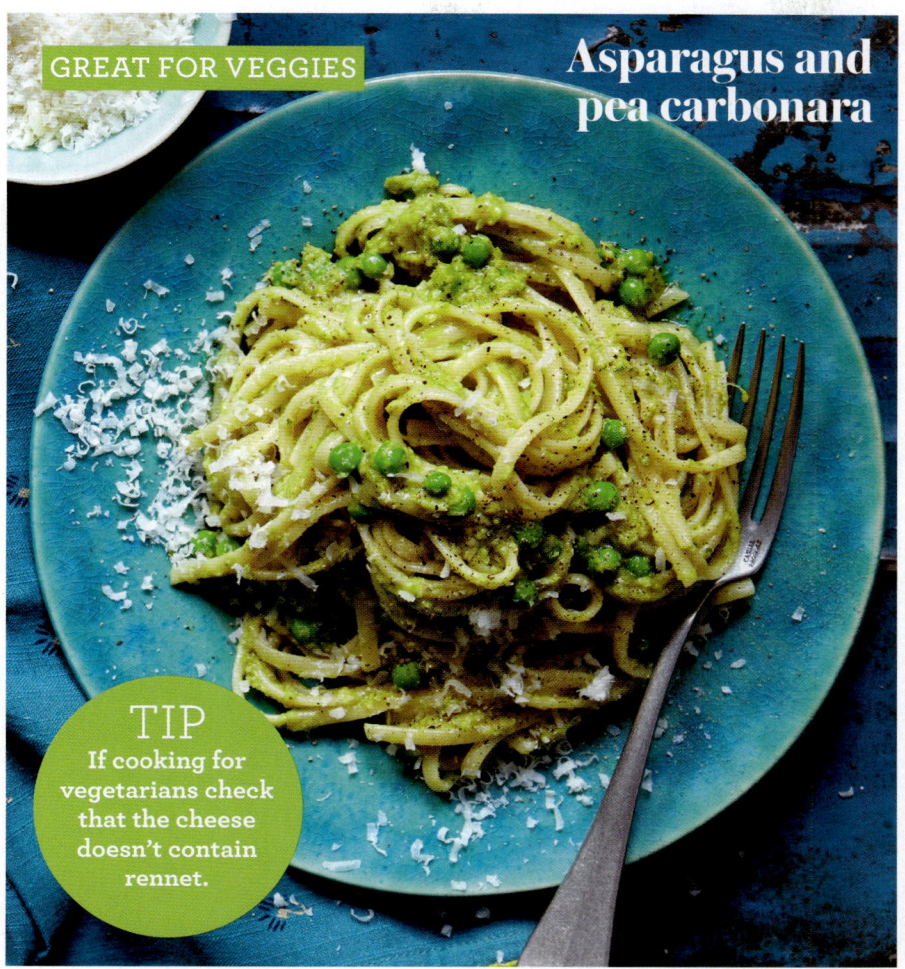

GREAT FOR VEGGIES
Asparagus and pea carbonara
TIP
If cooking for vegetarians check that the cheese doesn't contain rennet.

Asparagus and pea carbonara

Green up your carbonara with asparagus and peas for a new twist on a classic pasta dish

Serves 4 • Ready in 20 mins

400g (14oz) asparagus, cut into 3cm (1in) chunks
400g (14oz) dried linguine pasta
1 garlic clove, crushed
2 medium organic egg yolks
90g (3oz) unsalted butter
90g (3oz) Italian hard cheese, finely grated, plus extra to serve
1 bunch tarragon
100g (3½oz) petits pois, frozen

1 Bring a large pan of salted water to the boil, and blanch the asparagus for 2-3 mins. Remove with tongs and set aside, then add the pasta to the same water and cook according to the packet instructions.
2 In a blender, blitz the hot asparagus, garlic, egg yolks, butter, cheese and tarragon to a fine sauce, then set aside. In a small bowl, pour boiling water over the petits pois to defrost, then drain.
3 Toss the asparagus sauce through the drained, hot pasta, and then stir in the petits pois. Serve with the extra grated cheese.
Per serving: Cals 708, Fat 30g, Sat fat 17g, Carbs 77g

Asparagus and kale shakshuka

This Middle Eastern poached egg dish was crying out for asparagus

Serves 6 • Ready in 40 mins

100ml (3fl oz) olive oil
2 shallots, finely chopped
4 cloves garlic, crushed
1tsp each coriander and cumin seeds, toasted and ground
400g (14oz) tin chopped tomatoes
460g (16oz) jar roasted red peppers, drained and chopped
2 potatoes, diced
250g (9oz) asparagus, chopped into 5cm (2in) chunks
100g (3½oz) kale leaves, sliced or torn
6 large organic eggs
150ml (5fl oz) Greek yoghurt
Small bunch mint leaves, chopped
30g (1oz) shaved Italian-style hard cheese
2tbsp sesame seeds
Crusty bread, to serve

1 Heat the olive oil in a large frying pan. Add the shallots and cook for a few mins to soften, then stir in the garlic and spices. Cook for 2-3 mins. Blitz the tomatoes and peppers together with a stick blender, then stir into the shallot mixture. Add the diced potatoes and bring to a simmer. Cover and cook for 20 mins, stirring occasionally, until the liquid has reduced to a thick, rich sauce.
2 Stir in the asparagus and kale, and cook for 5 mins more, then make 6 wells in the sauce and crack an egg into each. Cover the pan and continue cooking until the eggs are cooked to your liking – 10-12 mins for medium-soft yolks.
3 Remove the frying pan from the heat. Dollop over the Greek yoghurt and top with the chopped mint, Italian-style hard cheese and sesame seeds. Serve straight away with crusty bread, to mop up the sauce.
Per serving: Cals 429, Fat 29g, Sat fat 7g, Carbs 23g

TIP
The perfect dish for a long weekend brunch.

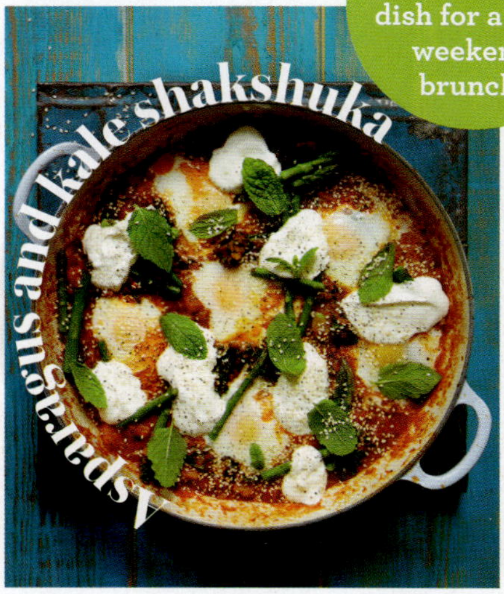
Asparagus and kale shakshuka

COMPILED BY: ROSE FOOKS. PHOTOS TI-MEDIACONTENT.COM

Gnocchi with ricotta and cauliflower

TIP This also works well with pasta shapes or filled tortellini instead of gnocchi.

A TASTE OF Spring

Easy ways to make fresh and tasty seasonal ingredients the star of your meal

A TASTE OF SPRING

Gnocchi with ricotta and cauliflower

Cauliflower florets pan-fried until toasted and golden are delicious tossed with pillowy soft potato dumplings and crispy bacon

Serves 4 • Ready in 25 mins

100g (3½oz) streaky bacon
2tbsp capers
25g (1oz) butter
1 cauliflower (approx 500g/17½oz), cut into florets
400g (14oz) gnocchi (find it in the pasta aisle)
100g (3½oz) shredded kale
250g (9oz) ricotta
Finely grated zest and juice of 1 lemon

1 Bring a large pan of water to the boil. At the same time, dry-fry the bacon in a large non-stick frying pan until crispy. Remove from the pan and set aside. Add the capers and butter to the bacon fat in the pan and fry for 2 mins until the capers are crispy. Remove and set aside with the bacon.
2 Add the cauliflower florets to the frying pan and fry for 5-10 mins until cooked through and slightly charred at the edges. While the cauliflower is cooking, add the gnocchi to the boiling water and cook following the instructions on the packet.
3 Stir the kale into the cauliflower with the ricotta and lemon zest and juice. Drain the gnocchi, add to the pan and stir to mix. Serve topped with the crispy bacon and capers.
Per serving: Cals 477, Fat 25g, Sat fat 13.5g, Carbs 37g

SEASONAL COOKBOOK woman&home 13

All-in-one lamb roast

TIP Cook courgettes, tomatoes and peppers in a separate roasting tin in the oven at the same time.

All-in-one lamb roast

Quicker and much less washing up than a traditional roast, what's not to love about this?

Serves 4 • Ready in 45 mins

750g (1lb 10oz) new potatoes, halved
400g (14oz) shallots, peeled
8 garlic cloves, unpeeled and lightly bashed
3 sprigs rosemary, leaves chopped, plus 3 sprigs
3tbsp olive oil
4 x 250g (9oz) boneless lamb rumps
4tsp Dijon mustard
50g (2oz) breadcrumbs
Grated zest of ½ lemon
½tsp dried oregano

1 Heat the oven to 220°C/425°F/Gas 7. Put the potatoes, shallots, garlic and rosemary sprigs in a large roasting tin. Drizzle with 2tbsp of the oil, season and mix well. Roast in the oven for 15 mins.
2 Meanwhile, roll the lamb rumps into mini-joint shapes and secure with cocktail sticks. Brown the meat all over in a hot pan then brush with the mustard.
3 Mix together the breadcrumbs, remaining oil, chopped rosemary, lemon zest and oregano and season. Press the crumbs onto the mustardy surface.
4 Turn the potatoes and shallots, add the lamb to the tin and cook for 20 mins (for medium) or 25-30 mins (for well done).
Per serving: Cals 670, Fat 32g, Sat fat 10g, Carbs 37g

Baked vanilla cheesecake with candied rhubarb

Ricotta and yoghurt lighten this classic cheesecake and the rhubarb topping is a match made in heaven

Serves 12 • Ready in 1 hr, plus cooling

For the base:
50g (2oz) butter, melted
125g (4½oz) light digestives, crushed
100g (3½oz) rough oatcakes, crushed
1tbsp honey
1tsp ground ginger
For the filling:
250g (9oz) ricotta
3 large eggs
8tbsp caster sugar
2tsp vanilla extract
3tbsp cornflour
200g (7oz) Greek yoghurt
400g (14oz) extra-light soft cheese
For the candied rhubarb:
200g (7oz) caster sugar
400g (14oz) rhubarb, thickly sliced diagonally
You will need:
A 22cm (8.6in) springform tin, oiled, and the base lined with baking paper

Baked vanilla cheesecake with candied rhubarb

A TASTE OF SPRING

Asparagus eggs Benedict

1 Heat the oven to 150°C/300°F/Gas 2. For the base, mix together the butter, digestives, oatcakes, honey and ginger and press into the base of the springform tin. Chill.
2 For the filling, in a food processor, whizz the ricotta and eggs together until smooth. Add the sugar, vanilla, cornflour, yoghurt and soft cheese and whizz again until smooth. Pour the mixture into the tin, place on a baking tray and bake for 50 mins, or until just set. Leave the cheesecake in the turned-off oven with the door open for 30 mins. Remove, leave to cool then chill for 3 hrs.
3 For the candied rhubarb, dissolve the sugar in 100ml (3½ fl oz) water in a pan over a low heat. Bring to the boil and bubble until syrupy. Add the rhubarb and poach for a few mins until just tender. Cool on a greaseproof-lined baking tray then spoon over the cheesecake to serve.
Per serving: Cals 418, Fat 14g, Sat fat 7g, Carbs 63g

Asparagus eggs Benedict

A delicious way to enjoy the new season's asparagus for brunch, lunch or dinner

Serves 2 • Ready in 15 mins

125g (4½oz) fine asparagus spears
1tbsp olive oil
2 large eggs
2 bagels
100ml (3½fl oz) ready-made hollandaise sauce from a jar, warmed
1 ripe avocado, sliced
1 lemon, halved

1 Heat a griddle or frying pan until hot. Toss the asparagus in the olive oil, season, and add to the pan. Cook, turning occasionally, for 3-4 mins until just tender and beginning to char.
2 At the same time, crack the eggs into a shallow pan of simmering water. Leave to poach gently for 4-5 mins until the white is set, but the yolk is still runny.
3 Split and toast the bagels. Spoon a little of the warmed hollandaise on to the bagel bases and top with avocado and asparagus. Remove the eggs from the pan with a slotted spoon, place on the asparagus and spoon the remaining hollandaise over the top. Add a squeeze of lemon juice, some black pepper and the other half of the bagel.
Per serving: Cals 884, Fat 67g, Sat fat 29g, Carbs 44g

TIP If you want to pack in the protein, why not add some smoked trout to your brunch?

SPRING

Pink grapefruit, black bean and rice salad

A zingy citrus salad to serve as a light lunch on its own or with chicken, fish or prawns

Serves 6 • Ready in 10 mins

2 large pink grapefruit
200g (7oz) packet cooked basmati rice
400g (14oz) can black beans, drained and rinsed
3tbsp extra virgin olive oil
4tbsp chopped fresh coriander

1 Over a bowl to catch the juice, segment the grapefruit using a small serrated knife, then squeeze out any remaining juice from the grapefruit.
2 Microwave the rice following packet instructions then mix it with the juice, fluffing the rice to separate.
3 Add the black beans, olive oil and coriander, stir well to mix and season. Top with the grapefruit segments to serve.
Per serving: Cals 160, Fat 6g, Sat fat 1g, Carbs 20g

> **TIP** Segmenting removes all the bitter white pith and membranes from grapefruit and oranges. Cut the skin (and pith) off the fruit in downward strokes, then cut between the membranes to release the segments

16 woman&home SEASONAL COOKBOOK

A TASTE OF SPRING

Pink grapefruit, black bean and rice salad

SPRING

Cod with miso butter

Halloumi, carrot and bean tacos

Cod with miso butter

Once you've tried this magical butter you'll be hooked – it gives everything a flavour boost in minutes

Serves 4 • Ready in 20 mins

4 x 175g (6oz) portions cod fillet
Tenderstem broccoli and baby new potatoes, to serve
For the miso butter:
200g (7oz) butter, softened
100g (3½oz) white miso paste
2tbsp lemon juice
2tsp grated lemon zest
2 spring onions, finely sliced

1 To make the miso butter, beat together the butter, miso paste, lemon juice, zest and spring onions.
2 Put the Tenderstem broccoli and potatoes on to cook and preheat the grill.
3 Spread a thick layer of the butter over the fish fillets and grill for 5-10 mins depending on the thickness of the fish, until just cooked through.
4 Toss the vegetables in any remaining butter and serve them with the cod.
Per serving: Cals 489, Fat 42g, Sat fat 26g, Carbs 3g

Halloumi, carrot and bean tacos

When you're home alone this makes a tasty light bite, but quantities can be easily increased to serve more if desired

Serves 1 • Ready in 10 mins

Light cooking spray
25g (1oz) reduced-fat halloumi cheese, cut into 2 slices
2 x 9cm (3½in) flour tortilla circles
1 small carrot, grated
2tbsp mixed beans in spicy tomato sauce, warmed
1tbsp frozen sweetcorn, defrosted and warmed
1 spring onion, finely sliced
A few mixed salad leaves and fresh coriander leaves

1 Heat a griddle pan or non-stick frying pan until hot. Spray the halloumi cheese with cooking spray and cook in the hot pan until warmed through.
2 In a separate frying pan, warm the tortilla circles over a high heat until they are toasted.

18 woman&home SEASONAL COOKBOOK

A Taste of Spring

TIP Dollop some crème fraîche on top of your puds to complement the sweet crumble and tart berries.

3 Mix together the carrot, beans, sweetcorn and most of the spring onion. Spoon the mixture on to the tortilla circles with the salad leaves and coriander. Top with the halloumi and scatter over the remaining spring onion slices, to serve.
Per serving: Cals 411, Fat 9g, Sat fat 4g, Carbs 61g

TIP For a vegan meal, use a dairy-free halloumi alternative such as Violife Mediterranean Style Block

Apple and blueberry cobbler

Enjoy this American twist on a fruit crumble with a golden buttermilk topping

Serves 5 • Ready in 55 mins

300g (10½oz) Bramley apples, peeled, cored and sliced
500g (15½oz) blueberries
60g (2½oz) golden caster sugar
1tbsp thickening granules
½tsp ground mixed spice
For the cobbler:
150g (4½oz) self-raising flour
60g (2½oz) butter, in small chunks
100g (3½oz) golden caster sugar
100ml (3½fl oz) buttermilk
1tbsp golden granulated sugar

1 Heat the oven to 200°C/400°F/Gas 6. Put the apples and blueberries into a buttered 1¼ (2pt) ovenproof dish. Sprinkle with the sugar, thickening granules and mixed spice.
2 To make the cobbler, put the flour into a food processor with the butter and then pulse for a few seconds until it forms crumbs. Add the caster sugar and buttermilk and blend briefly to form a soft dough.
3 Pull off pieces of the dough and arrange them on top of the fruit, but don't cover it completely. Sprinkle with a little granulated sugar and bake in the oven for 35-40 mins until the fruit is tender and bubbling and the topping is well risen and golden. Spoon into small dishes or cups, to serve.
Per serving: Cals 331, Fat 9g, Sat fat 5g, Carbs 60g

SPRING

Lamb en croûte with basil and mint stuffing

SERVE UP AN EASTER FEAST!

Serve up an EASTER FEAST!

Golden potato gratin

SPRING

TIP This also works well with other vegetables, such as purple sprouting broccoli.

VEGAN
DAIRY FREE

Crispy asparagus with maple syrup

Enjoy these with a glass of fizz to get things off to a good start

Serves 6 • Ready in 30 mins

100g (3½oz) plain flour
3tbsp cornflour
Salt and freshly ground black pepper
Finely grated zest of 1 lemon
3tbsp chopped tarragon
1tbsp ground coriander
250ml (8½fl oz) chilled sparkling water
Vegetable oil, for deep frying
250g (9oz) slim asparagus spears
Lime wedges and maple syrup

1 To make the batter, mix the flours together in a rectangular dish a little longer than the asparagus. Add a little salt and pepper, then stir in the lemon zest, tarragon and coriander. Stir in the chilled water, leaving the mixture quite lumpy.
2 Half fill a deep saucepan with oil and heat to 190°C/375°F/Gas 5, or until a drop of batter floats and sizzles as soon as it hits the oil.
3 Coat a few asparagus spears in batter, then lower them into the hot oil. Fry for 2-3 mins until golden and crisp. Remove with a slotted spoon and place on kitchen paper while you fry the rest.
4 Serve with a light scattering of salt, lime wedges and a small bowl of maple syrup for dipping.
Per serving: Cals 474, Fat 27g, Sat fat 6g, Carbs 12g

Courgette tart with feta

Flaky pastry filled with a silky cream filling

Serves 4 • Ready in 35 mins

250g (9oz) ricotta
Juice and zest of 1 lemon
4tbsp roughly chopped mint
4tbsp roughly chopped dill
375g (13oz) ready-rolled puff pastry
1 courgette, thinly sliced
200g (7oz) marrow, thinly sliced
40g (1½oz) vegetarian feta
1 egg yolk, mixed with 1tbsp milk
Salad, to serve
You will also need:
A flat baking tray, greased

1 Heat the oven to 200°C/400°F/Gas 6. Mix together the ricotta, lemon juice and zest and most of the herbs (reserve a few to serve) and season well. Unroll the pastry on to the baking tray and cut into 4 rectangles. Score a borderline 2½cm (1in) from the edge on all sides, making sure that you don't cut through the pastry. Spread the ricotta mixture over the pastry, leaving the outer border free from any toppings.
2 Top with slices of courgette and marrow and scatter over the feta, then brush the edges with the egg-yolk mix. Bake in the oven for 15-20 mins until crisp.
3 Scatter with the remaining herbs and serve with a mixed leaf salad on the side.
Per serving: Cals 513, Fat 34g, Sat fat 17g, Carbs 36g

TIP Scatter a handful of toasted pine nuts over the top before serving for added texture

22 woman&home SEASONAL COOKBOOK

SERVE UP AN EASTER FEAST!

GREAT FOR VEGGIES
MEAT FREE

Courgette tart with feta

Minted pea soup

Vibrant, light and quick to prepare

Serves 2 • Ready in 20 mins

½ small onion, chopped
1 garlic clove, crushed
50g (2oz) potato, cubed
500ml (17fl oz) vegetable stock
125g (4½oz) frozen peas
Several fresh mint leaves

1 Put the onion, garlic, potato and stock into a large pan. Bring to the boil and simmer for 5 mins.
2 Add the peas and most of the mint, return to the boil and simmer for 10 mins.
3 Pour into a food processor and blitz until smooth, season to taste and scatter a few mint leaves on top to serve.
Per serving: Cals 91, Fat 1g, Sat fat 0.4g, Carbs 13g

VEGAN
LOW CAL

TIP
If you make this ahead of time, chill it quickly to help retain the bright green colour, then reheat before serving.

SERVE UP AN EASTER FEAST!

Lamb en croûte with basil and mint stuffing

An impressive and delicious centrepiece for your Easter table

Serves 8 • Ready in 2 hrs 30 mins

1⅓kg (3lb) extra trimmed lamb, whole boneless leg
325g (11½oz) ready-rolled puff pastry sheet
1 egg, lightly beaten, to glaze
For the stuffing:
2 garlic cloves, sliced
2 slices white bread
100g (3½oz) pine nuts
3tbsp chopped mint
3tbsp chopped basil
2tbsp olive oil
2tbsp Dijon mustard
For the gravy:
150ml (5fl oz) Marsala
600ml (20fl oz) hot chicken stock
1tbsp sun-dried tomato paste
2tbsp thickening granules
Steamed vegetables, to serve

1 To make the stuffing, put the garlic, bread, pine nuts, mint, basil and seasoning in a food processor. Blitz to form crumbs. Add the oil and mustard. Blend to combine.
2 Heat the oven to 200°C/400°F/Gas 6. Season lamb generously and roast for 1 hr. Put a greased heavy based baking tray in the oven.
3 Unroll the pastry, cut off a strip from the longest end and cut into leaves, to decorate. Spoon the stuffing lengthways down the centre of the pastry. Position the lamb on top. Brush pastry edges with water and lift up and over the meat, pressing edges to seal. Upturn on to the preheated baking tray. Secure pastry leaves on top with water. Brush with beaten egg, to glaze. Bake for 1 hr, until pastry is golden and the meat is cooked through.
4 For the gravy, add the Marsala to the roasting tin with the meat juices and bubble for 1 min. Pour in the hot stock, and add the tomato paste. Heat until boiling, then whisk in the thickening granules. Serve with the lamb and steamed vegetables.
Per serving: Cals 579, Fat 35g, Sat fat 12g, Carbs 21g

TIP Make the stuffing ahead of time, as it can chill in the fridge for two days.

Golden potato gratin

The pancetta running through this gratin adds a beautiful salty flavour

Serves 8 • Ready in 1 hr 30 mins

2 x 77g (3oz) packs diced pancetta
2tsp sea salt
1tsp ground black pepper
1⅓kg (3lb) potatoes, peeled
400g (14oz) shallots, peeled
2tbsp chopped thyme leaves
300ml (10fl oz) vegetable stock
60g (2½oz) butter

1 Heat oven to 200°C/400°F/Gas 6. Pan-fry the pancetta until cooked. Drain the fat from the pancetta and use to grease a large ovenproof dish. Combine the sea salt and pepper in a small bowl and sprinkle some over the base of the ovenproof dish.
2 Fit a food processor with its slicing attachment. Push the potatoes through the tube to finely slice. Repeat to slice the shallots.
3 Stack the potato slices sideways, layering with shallots, pancetta, seasoning and thyme. Pour over the stock, dot with butter and cover with buttered foil. Bake for 40 mins. Uncover and cook for 20 more mins.
Per serving: Cals 272, Fat 13g, Sat fat 7g, Carbs 30g

татр TIP Cook the pancetta in a cold pan and gradually increase the heat to render fat.

Golden potato gratin

SEASONAL COOKBOOK **woman&home** 25

SPRING

MEAT FREE
LOW CAL

Spiced aubergine and courgette tabbouleh

TIP
You can use fresh chilli rather than the sauce. And toss on some toasted pumpkin seeds, too.

Spiced aubergine and courgette tabbouleh

Tabbouleh is a traditional Lebanese salad made with bulgur wheat, tomatoes and parsley. We've added slices of griddled courgette and aubergine to make it a little more substantial

Serves 6 • Ready in 25 mins

1 aubergine, trimmed and cut into 8 long slices
2 courgettes, trimmed, each cut into 4 slices
5tbsp olive oil
1tsp ground cinnamon
250g (9oz) bulgur wheat
Zest and juice of 1 lemon
1tbsp sweet chilli sauce
4 spring onions, trimmed and sliced
½ cucumber, deseeded and diced
6 tomatoes, deseeded and chopped
About 50g (2oz) parsley and mint
200g (7oz) pack feta cheese

1 Heat a griddle pan. Spread the slices of aubergine and courgette out on a tray. Mix the oil and cinnamon in a small bowl and brush this on both sides of the slices. Griddle in batches until browned and tender, keeping them warm in the oven as you go.
2 Meanwhile, put the bulgur wheat in a pan with 400ml (13½fl oz) cold water. Cover and bring to the boil, then simmer for 6 mins or until all the water has been absorbed. Transfer to a bowl.
3 Stir in the lemon zest and juice, chilli sauce, spring onions, cucumber and tomato. Chop the parsley and mint and stir it in with plenty of seasoning.
4 Arrange the aubergine and courgette slices on a large platter. Spoon the tabbouleh over and scatter with feta. Serve with lemon cheeks, if you like.
Per serving: Cals 369, Fat 17g, Sat fat 6g, Carbs 38g

Lemon cheesecake tart

If you have any room left after all that, enjoy a slice of this zesty cheesecake

Serves 8-10 • Ready in 1 hr 20 mins, plus chilling

250g (9oz) digestive biscuits
150g (5oz) unsalted butter
Grated zest of 1 lime
400g (14oz) cream cheese, at room temperature
150g (5oz) caster sugar
Finely grated zest of 2 lemons and 75ml (3fl oz) juice
3 medium eggs
Icing sugar, to serve
Blueberries, to serve
Thick double cream, to serve

1 Preheat the oven to 160°C/320°F/Gas 3. Grease a 6x20cm (2x8in) round spring-form tin.
2 In a food processor, blitz the biscuits to crumbs. Add the butter and lime zest and process until combined. Press the mixture into the base and up and around the side of the tin. Refrigerate for about 15 mins.
3 Meanwhile, beat the cream cheese, sugar and lemon zest together, until you get a smooth consistency. Add the eggs, one at a time, beating until well combined. Then, beat in the lemon juice, a little at a time, until the mixture is smooth.
4 Pour the mixture into the cake tin. Bake for 40-50 mins, until just set; the tart may still wobble slightly in the centre.
5 Leave the cheesecake to cool in the oven with the door slightly ajar, then refrigerate for around 4 hrs or until cold. Remove from the fridge and dust with icing sugar and top with blueberries, if using, before slicing and serving with a generous dollop of the cream.
Per serving: Cals 408-510, Fat 28-35g, Sat fat 16-20g, Carbs 32-40g

SERVE UP AN EASTER FEAST!

Lemon cheesecake tart

TIP For a variation on this dessert, add the zest of 3 limes and serve with strawberries.

EASTER SWEET TREATS

Easter sweet
TREATS

Celebrate Easter by delighting friends and family with one of our many show-stopping creations, such as our stunning stacked pavlova – or just enjoy a delicious bunny sandwich biscuit with a cuppa

You've heard of sourdough, but what about enriched dough? Try our recipes for an apple hot cross bun wreath or a wonderfully sticky chocolate babka cake

Savour rhubarb season with our comforting but sophisticated rhubarb and lavender puddings – they'll add a pop of pink to your Easter feast

SEASONAL COOKBOOK woman&home 29

SPRING

TIP Replace the white chocolate with dark for the icing if you like.

Triple-decker simnel cake

Triple-decker simnel cake

A contemporary take on an Easter classic

Serves 16 • Ready in 1 hr 15 mins, plus cooling

175g (6oz) butter, softened
350g (12oz) golden caster sugar
3 medium eggs
300g (10½oz) self-raising flour, sifted
¼tsp bicarbonate of soda
400ml (13½fl oz) buttermilk
25g (1oz) cocoa, sifted
50g (2oz) ground almonds
100g (3½oz) raspberries
2tsp pink food colouring gel
(we used Dr Oetker)
For the filling:
3tbsp chocolate spread
3tbsp raspberry jam
For the icing:
3 large egg whites
250g (9oz) caster sugar
200g (7oz) unsalted butter, cut into small cubes
200g (7oz) white chocolate, broken into squares
Pink stardust decorating lustre (available at Waitrose)
11 white chocolate truffles
You will need:
3 x 20cm (8in) round cake tins, greased and lined

1 Heat the oven to 180°C/350°F/Gas 4. Whisk the butter and sugar until fluffy. Whisk in the eggs. Fold in the flour, bicarb and buttermilk.
2 Divide the mixture into 3 bowls. Add the cocoa to one, and 25g (1oz) almonds to each of the other bowls. Lightly crush the raspberries with a fork and add to one of the bowls with almonds, along with the pink food colouring gel. Stir each bowl. Spoon the mixtures into the tins and bake for 25 mins until firm to the touch. Turn on to wire racks.
3 Put the chocolate cake on to a cake stand and spread over the chocolate spread. Top with the raspberry cake and spread with the jam. Finish with the almond cake.
4 For the icing, put the egg whites and sugar into a large bowl over a pan of simmering water. Stir until the sugar dissolves. Remove from the heat and whisk until it forms a thick meringue. Gradually add the butter, a cube at a time. Meanwhile, melt the chocolate and pour into the mixture while continuing to whisk.
5 Spread the icing over the top and sides of the cake, sprinkle with stardust and place the truffles on top.
Per serving: Cals 563, Fat 30g, Sat fat 16g, Carbs 52g

EASTER SWEET TREATS

Easter egg rocky road

You can never go wrong with a rocky road

Makes 16 • Ready in 20 mins, plus chilling

390g (14oz) milk chocolate
75g (3oz) butter
5tbsp golden syrup
200g (7oz) shortbread
50g (2oz) chocolate mini eggs
125g (4½oz) fudge
100g (3½oz) pink and white mini marshmallows
For the topping:
150g (5oz) milk chocolate
15g (½oz) butter
50g (2oz) fudge, chopped
50g (2oz) chocolate mini eggs
Hundreds and thousands
You will need:
An 18 x 28cm (7 x 11in) tin, greased and lined

1 To make the base, put the chocolate, butter and syrup into a bowl and melt over a pan of simmering water.
2 Meanwhile, crush the shortbread in a blender or with a rolling pin in a sturdy bowl. Put the mini eggs in a plastic bag and bash to crush. Cut the fudge into small pieces.
3 Take the chocolate off the heat, add the shortbread, fudge, crushed eggs and marshmallows. Mix well, then transfer to the tin and chill.
4 For the topping, melt the milk chocolate with the butter. Pour over the chilled base. Scatter over the fudge, mini eggs and hundreds and thousands, then chill until set. Cut into 16 even squares.
Per serving: Cals 450, Fat 24g, Sat fat 16g, Carbs 47g

TIP Dip a sharp knife in boiling water to make this easier to cut.

Easter egg rocky road

SEASONAL COOKBOOK **woman&home** 31

SPRING

Chocolate babka

This takes some time and effort to make, but is well worth every second (and calorie)

Serves 12 • Ready in 2 hrs, plus at least 5 hrs resting

120ml (4fl oz) milk
1 x 7g (0.2oz) sachet fast-acting yeast
300g (10½oz) strong white bread flour
1tsp salt
40g (1½oz) caster sugar
1 large egg
1tsp vanilla paste
70g (2½oz) butter, cut into 3cm (1in) cubes

For the filling:
120g (4oz) butter
80g (3oz) dark brown muscovado sugar
100g (3½oz) dark chocolate, melted
100g (3½oz) pecan nuts, roughly chopped

For the glaze:
50g (2oz) sugar

You will need:
A 500g (1lb) loaf tin

1 Heat the milk in a saucepan until warm – do not boil or simmer. Remove from the heat, pour into a jug and allow to cool slightly. Sprinkle over the yeast and leave for 5-10 mins until foamy.
2 In a mixer bowl, mix the flour, salt and sugar. In a small bowl, beat the egg and vanilla together. Add the milk and egg mixtures to the dry ingredients, mixing using a dough hook, and knead on a low speed until a smooth, elastic dough has formed. Beat in the cubes of butter a couple at a time, until the dough is smooth and slightly sticky. Cover the bowl with a wet cloth and leave at room temperature to prove for 5 hrs, or overnight, until doubled in size.
3 To make the filling, beat together all the ingredients except the pecans. Roll out the proved dough to form a 45 x 25cm (10 x 18in) rectangle. Spread the filling over the top, leaving a few cm around the border. Sprinkle over the nuts. From the long side of the rectangle, roll up the dough. Pinch together the edges to seal.
4 Cut down the length of the middle of the cylinder of dough, leaving about 5cm (2in) intact at one end. From this end, plait the two strands around each other, keeping the exposed filling facing up. Ease into the loaf tin, cover lightly with cling film and leave to rise for another 1½-2 hrs.
5 Preheat the oven to 170°C/325°F/Gas 3½, then bake for 45-50 mins – the dough should sound hollow when tapped.
6 To make the glaze, heat the sugar with 50ml (2fl oz) water in a pan until dissolved. Simmer for 5 mins and remove from the heat. Once the babka is out of the oven, brush over the glaze.
Per serving: Cals 485, Fat 14g, Sat fat 4g, Carbs 42g

TIP You can add any other nut to this mixture if you don't like pecans.

Chocolate babka

EASTER SWEET TREATS

Easter bunny melting moments

Children (and adults) will love these sandwich biscuit beauties

Makes 18 • Ready in 35 mins, plus cooling

220g (8oz) butter
90g (3oz) icing sugar
90g (3oz) cornflour
250g (9oz) plain flour
1tsp vanilla extract
For the filling:
100g (3½oz) softened butter
110g (4oz) icing sugar, sifted
2tbsp Nutella

1 Preheat the oven to 180°C/350°F/Gas 4. Beat together the butter and icing sugar until fluffy. Fold through the cornflour, plain flour and vanilla extract and stir until the mixture comes together.
2 Roll out on a floured surface to about 1½cm (½in) thick (if the dough tears, just press it together). Cut out bunny shapes with a cutter or knife – about 36 shapes to make 18 biscuits.
3 Bake for 12-15 mins until golden and crisp. Remove from the oven and allow to cool on a wire rack. Beat together the filling ingredients and spoon between the biscuits.
Per biscuit: Cals 243, Fat 16g, Sat fat 10g, Carbs 24g

Spiced chocolate cupcakes

These have a hint of spice and a delicious cream-cheese icing

Makes 12 • Ready in 40 mins, plus cooling

125g (4½oz) unsalted butter, softened
125g (4½oz) golden caster sugar
1tsp vanilla extract
2 large free-range eggs, beaten
100g (3½oz) plain flour
50g (2oz) cocoa powder, plus extra to dust
1tsp baking powder
¾tsp mixed spice
½tsp ground cinnamon
60g (2½oz) chopped candied orange peel
4tbsp milk
For the icing:
280g (10oz) full-fat Philadelphia cream cheese
100g (3½oz) unsalted butter, softened
100g (3½oz) icing sugar
Mini chocolate eggs and raspberries, to decorate

You will need:
12 cupcake cases
A 12-hole cupcake tin
A piping bag

1 Heat the oven to 180°C/350°F/Gas 4. Cream the butter and sugar for 10 mins until light, beat in the vanilla, then add the eggs and beat again to combine. Mix the flour, cocoa, baking powder and spices together, then sift into the cake mixture and fold until just combined. Stir in the candied peel and milk, then divide between the cupcake cases. Bake for 12-15 mins, then remove from the oven and allow to cool on a wire rack.
2 To make the icing, put half the cream cheese in a bowl with the butter and sieve over the icing sugar. Beat with an electric whisk until smooth. Add the remaining cream cheese, beat again and spoon into a piping bag.
3 Pipe the icing in swirls on to each cupcake, dust with cocoa and top with mini eggs and raspberries.
Per serving: Cals 350, Fat 23g, Sat fat 14g, Carbs 31g

TIP Make sure you leave the cakes to cool completely before you ice them, otherwise the icing may melt off the cake.

SPRING

TIP You can now buy cartons of egg whites from most supermarkets. Just make sure you split at least 3 eggs so you can use the yolks for the curd.

Meringue stack pavlova

Meringue stack pavlova

Make this super-easy dessert ahead to save on time

Serves 16 • Ready in 1 hr 30 mins, plus chilling

10 free-range egg whites
350g (12oz) caster sugar
1tbsp vanilla extract
1tbsp cornflour
1tbsp white wine vinegar

For the orange curd:
2 large oranges, zest and juice
3 egg yolks, 1 whole egg
90g (3oz) caster sugar
40g (1½oz) butter, cubed

To serve:
600ml (1pt) whipping or double cream
100g (3½oz) raspberries
100g (3½oz) blueberries
Mini chocolate eggs and edible flowers to decorate (optional)

1 Preheat the oven to 130°C/266°F/Gas ½. Beat the egg whites until thick and glossy, then slowly add the sugar, whisking continuously. Once the sugar has dissolved and the meringue forms thick peaks, whisk in the vanilla, cornflour and vinegar.
2 Spoon the meringue on to silicone mats or greased baking trays, to form 4 circles ranging from large to small. Place in the oven and bake for 1 hr 20 mins. Once cooked, open the oven door and allow to cool.
3 Meanwhile, for the curd, combine all the ingredients in a bowl and place over a pan of gently simmering water. Whisk for 20-25 mins until thickened. Chill.
4 To serve, whip the cream until soft peaks form. Sandwich the meringue layers together with the cream and orange curd and berries. Top with, and add to each layer, extra berries, flowers and mini eggs, if using. Serve immediately.
Per serving: Cals 310, Fat 19g, Sat fat 11g, Carbs 31g

TIP Did you know the redder the stalk of the rhubarb, the sweeter the flavour?

Lavender and vanilla custard pudding

These desserts are a great lighter option for the end of a meal

Serves 6 • Ready in 1 hr 15 mins, plus cooling

700g (1lb 8oz) rhubarb, cut into 3cm (1in) pieces
240g (8½oz) caster sugar
Grated zest and juice of ½ orange
550ml (18½fl oz) full-fat milk
5tbsp double cream
½tsp culinary lavender flowers
¼tsp vanilla paste or extract
1 egg
4 egg yolks
Icing sugar, to serve
You will need:
An ovenproof dish
6 x 150ml (5 fl oz) ramekins

1 Preheat the oven to 200°C/400°F/Gas 6. Place the rhubarb, 150g (5oz) of the caster sugar, the orange zest and juice in the dish and stir well to combine. Bake for 16-18 mins, until the rhubarb has started to soften. Set aside to cool, then strain (reserving the cooking liquor to use as a base for cocktails).
2 Reduce the oven temperature to 160°C/320°F/Gas 3. Heat the milk and cream with the lavender flowers and vanilla over a low heat until almost boiling, then set aside for 5 mins. Whisk the egg, yolks and remaining sugar together in a bowl, then pour in the milk mixture. Mix well, then strain into a jug.
3 Place the ramekins in a roasting tray. Divide the rhubarb between them, then pour in the custard. Pour boiling water into the tray so that it comes halfway up the sides of the ramekins. Bake in the oven for 25-30 mins until the custard is just set, but with a slight wobble in the middle. Remove from the oven and set aside to cool completely. Serve with a light dusting of icing sugar.
Per serving: Cals 317, Fat 12g, Sat fat 7g, Carbs 45

Hot cross bun bombes

A stunning Easter dessert that's so easy to make

Serves 6 • Ready in 1 hr, plus freezing

200g (7oz) raisins
4tbsp brandy
100g (3½oz) white marzipan
2 hot cross buns, finely crumbed
125g (4½oz) soft dark brown sugar
2 eggs, separated
250ml (8½fl oz) double cream
180ml (6fl oz) single cream
½tsp vanilla extract
½tsp mixed spice, plus extra to sprinkle
400g (14oz) can sliced peaches

You will need:
6 mini pudding moulds, lightly oiled and lined with cling film

1 Put the raisins and brandy in a pan and warm through. Leave for 10 mins for the raisins to plump up, then put in a blender with 3tbsp water and whizz until smooth.
2 Meanwhile, heat the oven to 200°C/400°F/Gas 6. Roll out the marzipan to the thickness of a £1 coin. Cut out 12 x 1cm-wide (⅓in) strips and lay them in the moulds across each other to create a cross in each mould.
3 Mix the hot cross bun crumbs with the sugar, spread out in a roasting tin and put in the oven for 5 mins to caramelise. Cool, then crush slightly.
4 Using an electric hand whisk, beat the egg yolks, creams, crumbs, vanilla and mixed spice until thickened and lightly whipped. Whisk the egg whites until soft peaks form and gently fold into the yolk mixture. Add the puréed raisins and fold through to give a rippled effect.
5 Spoon into the moulds, fold the marzipan strips and excess cling film over to cover, then freeze for 4 hrs. Transfer to the fridge for 15 mins before serving with sliced peaches and a sprinkle of mixed spice.
Per serving: Cals 634, Fat 32g, Sat fat 19g, Carbs 66g

TIP Alcohol free? Use orange juice instead of brandy.

Cinnamon and apple hot cross bun wreath

This festive wreath makes a big impression, and is perfect for tearing and sharing

Makes 20 • Ready in 1 hr 30 mins, plus 2 hrs 20 mins resting

300ml (10fl oz) full-fat milk
60g (2½oz) butter
500g (17½oz) strong white bread flour
1tsp salt
75g (3oz) golden caster sugar
7g (¼oz) sachet fast-action yeast
1 egg, lightly beaten
1tbsp sunflower oil
90g (3oz) sultanas
45g (1½oz) dried mixed peel
Finely grated zest of 1 orange
1 apple, peeled and grated
½tsp ground mixed spice
½tsp ground cinnamon

To finish
125g (4½oz) plain flour
3tbsp runny honey, to glaze

You will need:
A 30cm (12in) pizza tray
A recycled can, with label removed

1 Microwave the milk and butter for 1 min. Stir until the butter is melted.
2 Put the flour, salt, sugar and yeast in a bowl of a free-standing mixer fitted with a dough hook. Pour in the warm milk and butter, then add the egg. Mix on a slow speed into a sticky dough. Alternatively, mix with a wooden spoon. Continue mixing with the dough hook for 4 mins, or knead by hand for 6 mins, until the dough is smooth and elastic. Put in a clean, oiled bowl and cover with oiled cling film. Leave in a warm place for 1 hr or until doubled in size.
3 Remove the cling film and tip in the sultanas, peel, orange zest, apple and spices. Knead into the dough. Return the dough to the bowl, cover with oiled cling film and leave in a warm place to rise for 1 hr or until it has doubled in size.
4 Put the plain flour in a bowl and slowly add 75-100ml (2½-3fl oz) water to form a dough. Roll out on a floured surface and cut into 5mm x 10cm (¼-4in) strips.
5 Divide the dough into 20 pieces and shape into even rounds. Grease the pizza tray and can. Position the can upright in the centre of the tray and arrange the buns in 2 rows around it. Place the prepared strips in crosses on top of the buns, securing with water. Cover lightly with oiled cling film, and leave in a warm place for 20 mins, while the oven is warming to 220°C/425°F Gas 7.
6 Bake the wreath for 25-30 mins, turning if needed for even browning.
7 Add 1tbsp boiling water to the honey and use to glaze the buns as soon as they come out of the oven.
Per serving: Cals 200, Fat 4g, Sat fat 4g, Carbs 36g

TIP You can make, shape and freeze these, then cook from frozen for a fresh-baked taste without the last-minute fuss.

Cinnamon and apple hot cross bun wreath

SUMMER

38 woman&home SEASONAL COOKBOOK

Summer

42	Clotted cream madeleines	60	Pork tenderloin with onion salad
42	Strawberries and cream cake	62	Pesto potato salad
43	Balsamic strawberries and brown sugar mascarpone	63	Courgette and broccoli salad
		63	Sweet potato and sweetcorn salad
43	Strawberry and Campari sorbet	65	Planked salmon with nectarine salsa
46	Roast coriander chicken	65	Asian-style BBQ scallops
46	Clams with ginger and garlic	68	Chocolate mini cones
47	Baked mozzarella with prosciutto	68	Iced berry cheesecake
48	Rustic ratatouille tart	70	White chocolate popping candy cherries
48	Chilled noodles with prawns, mango and yuzu	70	Lemon poppy seed layer cake
51	Chicken salad	72	Raspberry mousse
51	Satay cashew chicken curry	73	Summer fruit tiramisu
54	Sardines with spinach in anchovy butter	74	Strawberry fool trifle
		74	Peaches in rosé
54	Sticky mustard lamb ribs	75	Lemon gin and tonic cheesecake
55	Chipotle chilli beef burgers	78	Roasted cherry tomato tart
57	Fragrant Asian salad with chicken	78	Picnic sandwich loaf
57	Thai spiced turkey burgers with Asian slaw	78	Watercress scones
		81	Middle Eastern couscous with feta
58	Summer bread salad	81	Broad bean hummus
58	Potato wedges with spiced sour cream dip	82	Spicy vegetable samosas
		82	Sharing Tex-Mex sausage roll

SUMMER

What's in SEASON

There's no better time of the year for fresh produce than summer. Fruit and veg are at their peak and it is also a great time for seasonal seafood. Tuck in!

✢ AVOCADOS
These are certainly a favoured fruit of the moment. The South African avocados are in season from July and are deliciously creamy. Try them mashed on toast with a sprinkling of chilli flakes and a squeeze of lemon, or paired with prawn cocktail for a fresh dinner.

✢ BEETROOT
Packed full of fibre, this versatile and colourful veg is great made into a variety of sides. Try roasted and tossed in honey at the last minute for a sweet addition to a summer roast dinner, or juice with carrots and ginger for a wake-up call.

✢ BROAD BEANS
There's something special about veg with a short season. If you grow your own, you'll have the benefit of being able to pick them while they're small, sweet and bursting with flavour. Blitz together with ready-made hummus for a posh twist on a classic.

✢ CUCUMBER
This is the perfect cooling summer ingredient. Pop slices in glasses of water, Pimm's or a G&T for a fresh hit. Alternatively, mix wedges up with a little salt, sugar and vinegar for a quick pickled side salad.

✢ NEW POTATOES
There's no better way to serve new potatoes than steamed, then tossed in butter or olive oil and finished with a good hit of salt and pepper.

✢ PEAS
Sweet and satisfying, peas in the UK have a short season, so you'd better snap them up while they're at their best. Try them fresh in salads or tossed through a vibrant curry.

✢ PEACHES
There's something so alluring about a soft, sweet-smelling peach. Use these beauties in fruit salads, pavlovas and trifles, or try roasting them with honey and pecans.

✢ RUNNER BEANS
These don't keep for long, and need to be so fresh that you could snap them and almost hear the crunch. If they're a bit stringy, use a potato peeler to peel away the strings, then slice horizontally and steam.

✢ TOMATOES
There's nothing more satisfying than a home-grown tomato. Store out of the fridge for the best flavour. Serve on garlic-rubbed toast with oil and basil for a speedy starter.

SEAFOOD

Mackerel, herring and sardines from our native waters are in plentiful supply in summer. For something fancier, try one of these shellfish options.

✢ **LOBSTER** Usually caught from June to September in the UK, British lobster is sweet and succulent. For a treat, try it grilled, served with garlic butter or lemon mayonnaise alongside a big pile of home-made chips!

✢ **CLAMS** Delicious, and a great source of zinc. Toss them through pasta with garlic, parsley, cherry tomatoes, a little chilli and some white wine. Alternatively, simply steam with cider and mop up all the juices with some crusty bread.

✢ **CRAB** Our native crabs come into their own in summer. Versatile crab is delicious in a watercress salad or on brown bread. Shellfish provide you with protein and vital minerals.

WHAT'S IN SEASON

STRAWBERRIES

It really is worth waiting for the British strawberry season, when they are at their sweetest and juiciest. Let them come to room temperature before eating. Serve with cream or turn the page for easy ideas...

SUMMER

Clotted cream madeleines

Madeleines aren't as tricky as you might think to make

Makes 18 • Ready in 30 mins

2 eggs
70g (2½oz) caster sugar
45g (1½oz) unsalted butter, softened, plus extra for greasing
45g (1½oz) clotted cream
2tsp runny honey
90g (3oz) plain flour, plus extra for dusting
½tsp baking powder
Strawberries, to serve

You will need:
A madeleine tin

1 Whisk the eggs and sugar together until expanded in volume. Beat in the butter, clotted cream and honey.
2 Sift in the flour and baking powder, and gently fold through.
3 Grease the madeleine tin well with butter and dust with flour. Spoon a little of the mixture in each.
4 Heat the oven to 180°C/350°F/Gas 4. Bake for 12 mins. Remove, cool for a minute then tip out onto a cooling rack. Serve with strawberries.
Per madeleine: Cals 83, Fat 4.5g, Sat fat 2.5g, Carbs 9.5g

Strawberries and cream cake

TIP To ensure you get an even stack, slice off the domed tops of each sponge.

Sometimes you can't beat a classic, and the simplicity of this strawberries and cream cake makes it a real showstopper. Try to have just one slice though...

Serves 12 • Ready in 1hr 10 mins, plus cooling

For the cake:
350g (12oz) self-raising flour
350g (12oz) caster sugar
350g (12oz) butter
6 eggs
2tsp baking powder
Splash of milk

For the filling and topping:
600ml (1pt) double cream
2tbsp icing sugar
3tbsp strawberry jam
400g (14oz) strawberries

You will need:
3 x 18cm (1 x 7in) round cake tins, greased and lined with baking paper

1 Heat the oven to 180°C/350°F/Gas 4. In a large mixing bowl, beat all the cake ingredients together.
2 Divide the mixture between the 3 tins and bake for 30 mins until golden and springy to touch. Leave to cool.
3 Make the cream by whisking the double cream and icing sugar together until softly peaking.
4 Stack the sponges with the cream and a little jam in between each layer, piped on if you like. Top with more cream, and strawberries.
Per serving: Cals 854, Fat 59g, Sat fat 37g, Carbs 73g

Clotted cream madeleines

42 woman&home SEASONAL COOKBOOK

Balsamic strawberries and brown sugar mascarpone

Quick and super simple, this delicious recipe celebrates the beauty of strawberries (almost) as they come

Serves 4 • Ready in 10 mins, plus macerating

600g (21oz) strawberries, hulled
1tbsp balsamic vinegar
1tbsp caster sugar
250g (9oz) mascarpone
50g (2oz) muscovado sugar

1 Roughly chop the strawberries and mix together with the balsamic vinegar and caster sugar, adding a crack of black pepper if desired. Leave to macerate for 30 mins.
2 Whisk together the mascarpone and muscovado sugar and serve with the strawberries.
Per serving: Cals 338, Fat 26g, Sat fat 18g, Carbs 21g

TIP You can tell how ripe strawberries are by smelling them – the sweeter the smell, the better the fruit!

Strawberry and Campari sorbet

This is a fruity scoop of goodness – a boozy celebration of summer strawberries that has a stylish Italian twist

Serves 10 • Ready in 15 mins, plus freezing

100ml (3½fl oz) lemon juice
250g (9oz) sugar
½ bunch basil
½tsp black pepper, cracked
450g (1lb) strawberry purée
100ml (3½fl oz) Campari

1 In a saucepan, gently heat the lemon juice with the sugar, 200ml (6fl oz) water, basil and pepper. As soon as the sugar has melted, remove from the heat and allow to cool. In a large bowl, mix together the strawberry purée and Campari. Remove the basil leaves and stir through the cooled sugar mixture.
2 Pour into a container, cover and freeze until solid. To serve, scoop balls of the sorbet into bowls.
Per serving: Cals 166, Fat 0g, Carbs 37g

SEASONAL COOKBOOK **woman&home** 43

SUMMER

A TASTE OF SUMMER

A taste of
SUMMER

Celebrate the arrival of summer with
some of the season's best flavours

Inspired by the freshest ingredients of the season,
this mouthwatering collection of recipes will bring
a dose of sunshine to any kitchen

These dishes work whether you're cooking
al fresco or the Great British weather
forces you back indoors

SUMMER

Rustic ratatouille tart

GREAT FOR VEGGIES

TIP This tart is a great way to use leftover roast veg.

Versatile ratatouille gets a makeover with this recipe, enclosed in a deliciously crisp pastry shell

Serves 4 • Ready in 2 hrs, plus chilling and cooling

320g (11oz) pack shortcrust pastry
2 medium courgettes, sliced
1 large aubergine, cubed
2 red peppers, cut into chunks
2tbsp olive oil
4 garlic cloves, thinly sliced
Small bunch basil leaves, torn
6 large eggs
125ml (4fl oz) milk
150g (5oz) goat's cheese log, broken into pieces
150g (5oz) baby plum tomatoes, halved

You will need:
20cm (8in) deep springform cake tin; baking paper; baking beans and 2 baking trays

1 Heat the oven to 190°C/375°F/Gas Mark 5. Roll out the pastry into a circle around the thickness of a £1 coin and use to line the cake tin – leaving the excess pastry. Prick the base and chill for at least 20 mins. Line with the baking paper and add the baking beans. Bake for 20 mins, then remove the beans and baking paper and cook for a further 10-15 mins until pale golden.
2 Meanwhile, place the vegetables on a baking tray. Drizzle over the oil, scatter over the garlic and season well. Toss everything together and roast for 30 mins, until the vegetables are tender and slightly charred at the edges. Stir through the basil leaves.
3 Turn down the oven to 180°C/350°F/Gas 4. Beat together the eggs and milk, seasoning well. Spoon half the vegetables, cheese and tomatoes into the pastry case, followed by half the egg mix. Add another layer of vegetables and egg mix, then top with the tomatoes and goat's cheese. Put on a baking tray and bake for 1 hr 20 mins, until just set and golden on top. Leave to cool for 15 mins before removing from the tin.
4 Serve warm, or bring to room temperature if chilling.
Per serving: Cals 751-500, Fat 51-34g, Sat fat 18.5-12g, Carbs 45-30g

Chilled noodles with prawns, mango and yuzu

Yuzu is an East Asian citrus fruit that you buy as a juice – it's a bit like lime juice crossed with something floral!

Serves 4 • Ready in 20 mins

300g (11oz) fine rice noodles
3tbsp toasted sesame oil
150g (5oz) broad beans
1 mango, cut into chunks
Small bunch coriander (around 25g/1oz), roughly chopped
4 spring onions, sliced
150g (5oz) king prawns
Juice of 1 lime
2tbsp yuzu juice

1 Cook the noodles according to the pack instructions. Refresh under cold, running water, transfer to a serving dish and toss through 1tbsp of the sesame oil.
2 Blanch and pod the broad beans and add to the noodles with the mango, coriander, half the spring onions and all the prawns.
3 Combine the lime juice, yuzu and remaining sesame oil, and pour over the salad. Mix well. Scatter over the remaining spring onions and serve.
Per serving: Cals 460, Fat 9g, Sat fat 1.5g, Carbs 71g

Yuzu juice was hard to find in the UK just a few years ago, but is now available in big supermarkets

Chilled noodles with prawns, mango and yuzu

TIP
The salad will keep for a day in the fridge – just add the coriander and spring onions to serve.

LOW CAL

SUMMER

Satay cashew chicken curry

TIP
To freeze this dish, reduce the cooking time by 5 mins and complete the recipe to the end of step 2. Cool the chicken then freeze in a lidded container for up to 1 month. Defrost overnight in the fridge. Return to a heavy-based casserole and slowly heat through until piping hot, then complete stage 3.

LOW CAL

A TASTE OF SUMMER

Satay cashew chicken curry

This delicious, fragrant stew can also be made with peanut butter

Serves 6 • Ready in 45 mins

2tsp rapeseed oil
6 chicken breasts, cut into chunks
For the cashew sauce:
2 banana shallots, chopped
5 garlic cloves, crushed
1 red chilli, seeds removed, finely chopped
100g (3½oz) cashew nut butter
200ml (6fl oz) can coconut milk
100ml (3fl oz) coconut water
1tsp honey
½tsp fish sauce
Zest and juice of 1 lime
150g (5oz) tatsoi or pak choi, bottom stalks removed
To garnish:
1 chilli, finely sliced
4 spring onions, finely sliced
1tbsp coconut flakes
2tbsp cashew nuts, roughly chopped
1tbsp coriander leaves

1 Heat the oil in a heavy-based casserole pan over a medium heat and brown the chicken on all sides. Remove from the pan and set aside. Put the shallots, garlic and chilli in the pan and cook gently for 5 mins, until the shallots are soft.
2 Return the chicken to the pan, along with the cashew nut butter, coconut milk, coconut water, honey and fish sauce, and cook on a medium heat for 20 mins or until the chicken is cooked through.
3 Stir in the tatsoi or pak choi and heat for 1 min. Top with all the garnishes and serve with rice noodles or basmati rice.
Per serving: Cals 400, Fat 22g, Sat fat 10g, Carbs 8g

TIP This salad is also delicious using chargrilled pork tenderloin.

LOW CAL

Chicken salad

There are a lot of ingredients in the dressing, but it's worth the effort for the perfect balance of flavours

Serves 4 • Ready in 35 mins

For the dressing:
1 banana shallot, chopped
3 garlic cloves, crushed
½ red chilli, seeds removed and finely chopped
50g (2oz) cashew nut butter
½ x 200ml (6fl oz) can coconut milk
50ml (1½fl oz) coconut water
½tsp honey
A dash of fish sauce
Zest and juice of ½ lime
For the salad:
2 baby gem hearts, ends trimmed and quartered
4 small chicken breasts
3tsp rapeseed oil
½ cucumber, ribboned
¼ red cabbage, finely sliced
100g (3½oz) cherry tomatoes, halved
140g (5oz) bag mixed leaf salad
2tbsp cashew nuts
1tbsp coconut flakes

1 Whisk all the dressing ingredients together and season well. Set aside.
2 Heat a griddle pan over a high heat. Brush the baby gem then the chicken with the oil. Griddle the lettuce for 30 secs - 1 min per side. Griddle the chicken; heat for a few mins until cooked through, turning halfway.
3 Slice the cooked chicken then add to a large bowl with the cucumber, cabbage, tomatoes, mixed leaves, cashews and coconut flakes. Drizzle with the dressing and serve.
Per serving: Cals 406, Fat 22g, Sat fat 9g, Carbs 12g

Sticky mustard lamb ribs

Great value but, like all ribs, they need slow cooking before you crisp them up on the grill

Serves 4 • Ready in 2 hrs 20 mins, plus marinating

For the master barbecue rub:
25g (1oz) smoked paprika
25g (1oz) sea salt
½tbsp mild or hot chilli powder
1tbsp crushed coriander seeds
1½tbsp freshly ground black pepper
1½tbsp soft brown sugar
For the lamb:
2tbsp Dijon mustard
2tbsp maple syrup
2 sheets of lamb ribs (or have your butcher cut them up first)
You will need:
A few handfuls of soaked wood chips (optional)

1 Mix together the barbecue rub. Add the mustard and maple syrup, mix, then spread over the meaty side of the ribs. Now you can marinate them for a few hours if you like.
2 Heat the oven to 150°C/300°F/Gas 2. Put the ribs into a roasting tin and cover with foil. Bake for 2 hours.
3 When you're ready to serve, prepare your barbecue. Add your wood chips to the hot coals if you are using them. Cook the ribs for around 15 mins, when they should be browned and crispy.
Per serving: Cals 450, Fat 30g, Sat fat 14g, Carbs 1.5g

> TIP **If you can, you'll get this dish at its best by marinating the lamb overnight to intensify the flavour**

Sardines with spinach in anchovy butter

This is the perfect recipe for a fish lover's BBQ and will make you feel like you are by the sea wherever you are. Serve with crusty bread

Serves 4 • Ready in 15 mins

75g (3oz) softened unsalted butter
25g (1oz) chopped anchovy fillets
16 sardines
1tbsp olive oil
400g (14oz) spinach
Lemon wedges, to serve

1 Blend the butter with the anchovies. Dry 16 sardines and toss in the oil. Place in an oiled fish grill, sprinkle with sea salt and barbecue for 2 mins on each side.
2 Heat the anchovy butter in a pan, add the spinach and sauté for 3 mins. Serve with the lemon wedges.
Per serving: Cals 450, Fat 30g, Sat fat 14g, Carbs 1.5g

> TIP Make the anchovy butter a day in advance and keep it sealed in the fridge until you need it.

DAIRY FREE, GLUTEN FREE

A TASTE OF SUMMER

Satay cashew chicken curry

This delicious, fragrant stew can also be made with peanut butter

Serves 6 • Ready in 45 mins

2tsp rapeseed oil
6 chicken breasts, cut into chunks
For the cashew sauce:
2 banana shallots, chopped
5 garlic cloves, crushed
1 red chilli, seeds removed, finely chopped
100g (3½oz) cashew nut butter
200ml (6fl oz) can coconut milk
100ml (3fl oz) coconut water
1tsp honey
½tsp fish sauce
Zest and juice of 1 lime
150g (5oz) tatsoi or pak choi, bottom stalks removed
To garnish:
1 chilli, finely sliced
4 spring onions, finely sliced
1tbsp coconut flakes
2tbsp cashew nuts, roughly chopped
1tbsp coriander leaves

1 Heat the oil in a heavy-based casserole pan over a medium heat and brown the chicken on all sides. Remove from the pan and set aside.
Put the shallots, garlic and chilli in the pan and cook gently for 5 mins, until the shallots are soft.
2 Return the chicken to the pan, along with the cashew nut butter, coconut milk, coconut water, honey and fish sauce, and cook on a medium heat for 20 mins or until the chicken is cooked through.
3 Stir in the tatsoi or pak choi and heat for 1 min. Top with all the garnishes and serve with rice noodles or basmati rice.
Per serving: Cals 400, Fat 22g, Sat fat 10g, Carbs 8g

Chicken salad

LOW CAL

TIP This salad is also delicious using chargrilled pork tenderloin.

Chicken salad

There are a lot of ingredients in the dressing, but it's worth the effort for the perfect balance of flavours

Serves 4 • Ready in 35 mins

For the dressing:
1 banana shallot, chopped
3 garlic cloves, crushed
½ red chilli, seeds removed and finely chopped
50g (2oz) cashew nut butter
½ x 200ml (6fl oz) can coconut milk
50ml (1½fl oz) coconut water
½tsp honey
A dash of fish sauce
Zest and juice of ½ lime
For the salad:
2 baby gem hearts, ends trimmed and quartered
4 small chicken breasts
3tsp rapeseed oil
½ cucumber, ribboned
¼ red cabbage, finely sliced
100g (3½oz) cherry tomatoes, halved
140g (5oz) bag mixed leaf salad
2tbsp cashew nuts
1tbsp coconut flakes

1 Whisk all the dressing ingredients together and season well. Set aside.
2 Heat a griddle pan over a high heat. Brush the baby gem then the chicken with the oil. Griddle the lettuce for 30 secs - 1 min per side. Griddle the chicken; heat for a few mins until cooked through, turning halfway.
3 Slice the cooked chicken then add to a large bowl with the cucumber, cabbage, tomatoes, mixed leaves, cashews and coconut flakes. Drizzle with the dressing and serve.
Per serving: Cals 406, Fat 22g, Sat fat 9g, Carbs 12g

SUMMER

Fire up *the* BBQ!

The al fresco entertaining season is finally in full swing and we've got a whole host of delicious recipes to help you put on a sizzling feast

FIRE UP THE BBQ!

SEASONAL COOKBOOK woman&home 53

Sticky mustard lamb ribs

Great value but, like all ribs, they need slow cooking before you crisp them up on the grill

Serves 4 • Ready in 2 hrs 20 mins, plus marinating

For the master barbecue rub:
25g (1oz) smoked paprika
25g (1oz) sea salt
½tbsp mild or hot chilli powder
1tbsp crushed coriander seeds
1½tbsp freshly ground black pepper
1½tbsp soft brown sugar
For the lamb:
2tbsp Dijon mustard
2tbsp maple syrup
2 sheets of lamb ribs (or have your butcher cut them up first)
You will need:
A few handfuls of soaked wood chips (optional)

1 Mix together the barbecue rub. Add the mustard and maple syrup, mix, then spread over the meaty side of the ribs. Now you can marinate them for a few hours if you like.
2 Heat the oven to 150°C/300°F/Gas 2. Put the ribs into a roasting tin and cover with foil. Bake for 2 hours.
3 When you're ready to serve, prepare your barbecue. Add your wood chips to the hot coals if you are using them. Cook the ribs for around 15 mins, when they should be browned and crispy.
Per serving: Cals 450, Fat 30g, Sat fat 14g, Carbs 1.5g

TIP **If you can, you'll get this dish at its best by marinating the lamb overnight to intensify the flavour**

TIP Make the anchovy butter a day in advance and keep it sealed in the fridge until you need it.

Sardines with spinach in anchovy butter

This is the perfect recipe for a fish lover's BBQ and will make you feel like you are by the sea wherever you are. Serve with crusty bread

Serves 4 • Ready in 15 mins

75g (3oz) softened unsalted butter
25g (1oz) chopped anchovy fillets
16 sardines
1tbsp olive oil
400g (14oz) spinach
Lemon wedges, to serve

1 Blend the butter with the anchovies. Dry 16 sardines and toss in the oil. Place in an oiled fish grill, sprinkle with sea salt and barbecue for 2 mins on each side.
2 Heat the anchovy butter in a pan, add the spinach and sauté for 3 mins. Serve with the lemon wedges.
Per serving: Cals 450, Fat 30g, Sat fat 14g, Carbs 1.5g

DAIRY FREE, GLUTEN FREE

FIRE UP THE BBQ!

Chipotle chilli beef burgers

DAIRY FREE, GLUTEN FREE

TIP These burgers can be frozen for up to a month. Defrost in the fridge overnight before continuing with step 2.

Chipotle chilli beef burgers

The kidney beans bulk out the meat for a really punchy burger

Makes 6 • Ready in 25 mins, plus chilling

400g (14oz) can kidney beans, rinsed
500g (1lb) beef steak mince
1½tbsp tomato purée
2 garlic cloves, crushed
1 large free-range egg yolk
10 cornichons, very finely chopped
A large handful of coriander leaves, finely chopped
1-2tsp dried crushed chipotle chilli or chipotle paste
¼tsp sweet smoked paprika
1tbsp sunflower oil

1 Mash up the kidney beans with a fork. Put all the ingredients except the oil in a large bowl and use your hands to mix well. Divide into 6 equal portions then shape into burgers. Cover and set aside in the fridge to firm up for at least 2 hrs or overnight. You need them to firm up well or they may fall apart on the grill.
2 Prepare your barbecue for direct heat, brush the burgers lightly with the oil and cook for around 4 mins on each side or until cooked through. Serve on a bun, if you like, with guacamole and tortilla chips.
Per serving: Cals 231, Fat 13g, Sat fat 5g, Carbs 8g

SEASONAL COOKBOOK **woman&home** 55

SUMMER

TIP
Japanese rice vinegar makes a delicious fat-free salad dressing all on its own.

Fragrant Asian salad with chicken

DAIRY FREE

FIRE UP THE BBQ!

Fragrant Asian salad with chicken

Serves 6 to 8 • Ready in 25 mins

Simple, light and fresh, this salad can be prepared ahead – just leave it in the fridge for a couple of hrs before serving

800g (28oz) mini chicken fillets
1tbsp oil
Juice 1 lime
2tbsp light soy sauce
2tbsp Thai fish sauce
2tbsp palm sugar or light brown sugar
4tbsp Japanese rice vinegar
500g (1lb) cooked basmati rice
250g (9oz) pineapple chunks, chopped
1 red chilli, finely chopped
4 spring onions, finely sliced
Large handful mint leaves, roughly chopped
Large handful coriander leaves, roughly chopped

1 For the chicken, heat a griddle pan to hot. Brush the chicken lightly with the oil, season with salt and pepper and cook them in batches for 3 to 4 mins on each side or until cooked through.
2 For the dressing, mix the lime juice, soy sauce, fish sauce, sugar and vinegar until combined. Place the rice, pineapple, red chilli and spring onions in a large bowl and toss through the dressing. To serve, stir in the herbs and serve the chicken on the side.
Per serving: Cals 318, Fat 4.5g, Sat fat 1g, Carbs 34g

TIP Don't swap in Western vinegar for the rice one – you'll get a very different effect!

Thai spiced turkey burgers with Asian slaw

LOW CALORIE, GLUTEN FREE

Thai spiced turkey burgers with Asian slaw

Ditch the red meat and try these light and spicy satisfying bites

Makes 6 • Ready in 40 mins, plus chilling

2 large shallots
4 garlic cloves, crushed
2 green chillies, roughly chopped
2 lemongrass stalks, trimmed, outer layer removed, roughly chopped
2tsp Thai fish sauce
1tbsp sunflower oil
1kg (2lb) turkey mince
4 spring onions, trimmed, chopped
For the slaw:
2cm (¾in) root ginger, finely grated
3tbsp mayonnaise
3tbsp natural yoghurt
2tsp sesame oil
2tbsp rice wine vinegar
½tsp sea salt
1 large shallot, peeled and sliced
2 large carrots, cut into thin sticks
½ white cabbage, finely sliced
Large handful of coriander, chopped
1tsp toasted sesame seeds

1 In a food processor, blend the shallots, garlic, chilli, lemongrass and fish sauce with ½ the oil until smooth; set aside. Mix the mince with the paste and spring onions; season. Divide into 6 patties (or 12 mini ones), place on a baking tray, covered, and leave in the fridge for at least 1 hr, or overnight, to firm up.
2 For the slaw, mix the ginger, mayo, yoghurt, oil, vinegar and salt in a large bowl until smooth. Add the veg, toss well to coat and set aside for at least 1 hr. When ready to serve, toss with the coriander and sesame seeds.
3 Heat the oven to 200°C/400°F/Gas 6. Heat a griddle to hot. Brush the burgers with the remaining oil and fry on each side for 1 or 2 mins, or until browned. Remove to a baking tray and cook in the oven for 12 to 15 mins, or cook on the barbecue. Serve with burger buns, sliced tomatoes and the slaw.
Per burger: Cals 352, Fat 12g, Sat fat 2.5g, Carbs 30g

SUMMER

Summer bread salad

This is a good way of using up bread that's a little stale! Sourdough does have more flavour than most breads but it's not crucial to use it here

Serves 6-8 • Ready in 10 mins, plus soaking

150ml (5fl oz) extra virgin olive oil
50ml (2oz) red wine vinegar
2 garlic cloves, crushed
250g (9oz) sourdough bread, torn into small pieces
250g (9oz) broad beans, podded and shelled
400g (14oz) tomatoes, chopped
1 cucumber, chopped
8 radishes, chopped
1 roasted red pepper, roughly chopped
Small handful flat-leaf parsley, chopped
Small handful basil leaves, chopped

1 Mix the oil with the red wine vinegar, garlic and plenty of seasoning. Move to a bowl with the bread chunks and toss to coat. Leave to soak for an hr – the bread should be moist but not soggy.
2 When ready to serve, add the vegetables and herbs to the bread and toss well.
Per serving: Cals 315-236, Fat 20-15g, Sat fat 3-2g, Carbs 26-20g

TIP This recipe would also work brilliantly with sweet potatoes – which count as one of your 5 a day.

Potato wedges with spiced sour cream dip

Home-made wedges are so much more satisfying than shop-bought and they're easy to make too!

Serves 6 • Ready in 45 mins

900g (2lb) potatoes, scrubbed and cut into wedges
3tbsp olive oil
2tsp smoked paprika
1tbsp cumin seeds, lightly crushed
300g (10½oz) soured cream
Zest 2 limes
Small handful flat-leaf parsley, finely chopped

1 Heat the oven to 200°C/400°F/Gas 6. For the wedges, toss them in 2tbsp oil, the paprika and some sea salt. Spread on to a baking tray and cook for 40 mins or until cooked through.
2 For the dip, heat the remaining oil in a small pan, add the cumin seeds and toast for 1 min then set aside to cool. In a bowl, mix together the toasted cumin seeds, the oil from the pan, soured cream and the lime zest. Toss the wedges in the parsley and some sea salt before serving with the dip.
Per serving: Cals 264, Fat 16g, Sat fat 7g, Carbs 26g

58 woman&home SEASONAL COOKBOOK

FIRE UP THE BBQ!

Summer bread salad

TIP Soak the bread ahead of time so you can throw the salad together just before you need it.

Smoked hickory chicken wings

TIP Make the marinade up to a day in advance, keeping it covered in the fridge.

Smoked hickory chicken wings

Everyone loves a chicken wing and now you can buy free-range ones, even better. These are bang on-trend with the fashion for smoky food

Serves 6 to 8
Ready in 35 mins, plus marinating

24 chicken wings
For the marinade:
2tbsp dark muscovado sugar
1tbsp red wine vinegar
1tbsp Worcestershire sauce
1tsp mustard powder
150g (5oz) tomato ketchup
1tbsp+2tsp water
¼tsp chilli powder
½tsp garlic salt
OR 250g (9oz) barbecue sauce
You will need:
A large handful hickory chips, soaked, in water

1 If you're making the barbecue sauce, mix all the marinade ingredients to form a smooth paste. Place the chicken in a bowl and cover with the marinade. Mix well to coat, cover and put in the fridge for a few hrs or overnight to marinate.
TO BARBECUE
For the barbecue, simply add the soaked hickory chips to the barbecue with the coals. Start cooking the wings on the hot spot of the coals then move to a cooler spot to cook through, for around 15 to 20 mins.
TO OVEN COOK
Heat the oven to 200°C/400°F/Gas 6. Place the hickory chips in a roasting tin, and add a wire rack. Cover with a tent of foil, sealing the edges. Heat and allow smoke to develop, for around 10 mins. Remove the foil, take the chicken out of the marinade and place directly on the wire rack. Re-cover with the foil and cook for 25 to 30 mins.
Per serving: Cals 532-399, Fat 31-23g, Sat fat 9-6.5g, Carbs 11-8.5g

SUMMER

Spicy mushroom and halloumi burgers

GREAT FOR VEGGIES

TIP Marinate the mushrooms a day ahead to really get the flavour in and they will be ready when you need them.

Spicy mushroom and halloumi burgers

This East meets West dish might seem a strange flavour combination but it all goes together perfectly for a really filling burger

Makes 6 • Ready in 35 mins, plus marinating time

4 garlic cloves, crushed
4cm (1½in) fresh ginger, finely grated
4 cardamom pods, seeds removed and crushed
2tsp ground cumin
2tsp ground coriander
¼-½tsp chilli powder
Good pinch ground cloves
½tsp turmeric
¼tsp paprika
Good squeeze lemon juice
250g (9oz) natural yoghurt
6 portobello mushrooms
400g (14oz) halloumi, cut into 6 slices

1 Mix the garlic, ginger, spices, lemon juice and yoghurt in a large bowl until smooth, season then add the mushrooms to the bowl. Coat well in the mixture then leave to marinate for 30 mins to 2 hrs.
2 Heat the oven to 220°C/425°F/Gas 7. Place the mushrooms on a lined baking tray and put a slice of halloumi on top of each, then cook in the oven for 20 to 25 mins. Serve in burger buns with mango chutney and a crunchy salad.
Per serving: Cals 251, Fat 18g, Sat fat 12g, Carbs 10g

Pork tenderloin with onion salad

Sticky, spicy and citrussy with a fresh kick from the pomegranate – this is bound to become a favourite

Serves 6 • Ready in 40 mins, plus marinating

3tbsp pomegranate molasses
1tbsp maple syrup or honey
900g (2lb) pork tenderloin
1tbsp oil
4 medium onions, cut into wedges
2tbsp lemon juice
75g (3oz) rocket
Large handful flat-leaf parsley, chopped
2tsp sumac
110g (4oz) pack fresh pomegranate seeds

1 Mix the pomegranate molasses with the maple syrup, then use this to coat the pork, season and leave for a few hrs or overnight.
2 Heat the oven to 200°C/400°F/Gas 6. Heat ½ the oil in a frying pan then sear all sides of the pork. Place in a roasting tin lined with foil along with the remaining marinade and the onions. Drizzle over the remaining oil and roast for 30 mins.
3 To serve, place the onion wedges on a serving dish, and drizzle over the lemon juice. Add the rocket, parsley and sumac. Slice the pork, place on the salad, add the pan juices and scatter over the pomegranate seeds.
Per serving: Cals 265, Fat 8g, Sat fat 2.5g, Carbs 14g

TIP If you can't get Pomegranate molasses, use Pomegranate juice and sugar instead

FIRE UP THE BBQ!

DAIRY FREE
LOW CALORIE
GLUTEN FREE

Pork tenderloin with onion salad

SUMMER

Pesto potato salad

Every barbecue needs a spud – dress the potatoes while warm to absorb the dressing

Serves 4 to 6 •
Ready in 25 mins

750g (1lb 10oz) baby new potatoes
125g (4½oz) shelled edamame beans
125g (4½oz) peas
175g (6oz) baby broad beans
2tbsp mayonnaise
3tbsp fresh pesto
½tbsp lemon juice large handful basil leaves

1 Bring the potatoes to the boil in a pan of salted water, simmer until tender then drain.
2 Meanwhile, bring a pan of water to the boil. Add the edamame beans, peas and broad beans, remove from the heat and leave for 2 mins. If frozen, drain and rinse under cold water. Shell the broad beans then set all aside. In a large bowl, mix the mayo, pesto and lemon juice until combined, season with black pepper, add the potatoes while still warm and mix well to coat. Stir in the beans, peas and basil leaves once cooled.
Per serving: Cals 350-231, Fat 15.5-10.5g, Sat fat 1.5-1g, Carbs 39-26g

TIP If serving for veggies, make sure that the pesto uses an alternative to Parmesan

GLUTEN FREE

Pesto potato salad

Sweet potato and sweetcorn salad

TIP If you like spice, try adding some finely chopped red chilli for a bit of a kick.

TIP The smallest capers available, non-pareil are more delicate in texture with a more intense flavour.

GLUTEN FREE
GREAT FOR VEGANS

Courgette and broccoli salad

Courgette and broccoli salad

This simple salad is packed with crunch and flavour. Use large courgettes as they're easier to ribbon peel

Serves 6 to 8 • Ready in 20 mins

500g (1lb) courgettes
400g (14oz) Tenderstem broccoli
3tbsp small (non-pareil) capers
2tbsp white wine vinegar
4tbsp extra virgin olive oil

1 Peel the courgettes into ribbons with a peeler. Place in a bowl and season well. Blanch the broccoli in boiling water for 2 mins then refresh under the cold tap. Add the capers, vinegar and oil and mix well.
Per serving: Cals 107-80, Fat 8-6g, Sat fat 1.3-1g, Carbs 3-2g

Sweet potato and sweetcorn salad

No dressing required – just a squeeze of fresh lime is all you need

Serves 4 to 6 • Ready in 45 mins

1¼kg (3lb) sweet potatoes, peeled and cut into large chunks
1tbsp sunflower oil
4 sweetcorn cobs
2 ripe avocados
Good squeeze of lime juice

1 Heat the oven to 200°C/400°F/Gas 6. Put the sweet potatoes into a roasting tin, add the oil and toss well. Season and roast for 35 mins or until it's just tender.
2 Stand the sweetcorn cobs upright and, using a sharp knife, strip the corn from the cob vertically.
3 Heat a frying pan to medium-high and cook the sweetcorn for 4 or 5 mins, or until browned and tender.
4 Cut the avocado into wedges and toss in the lime juice, then mix with the rest of the ingredients, season and serve.
Per serving: Cals 533-355, Fat 20-13.5g, Sat fat 4.5-3g, Carbs 81-54g

Planked salmon with nectarine salsa

DAIRY FREE
GLUTEN FREE
LOW CALORIE

Planked salmon with nectarine salsa

Cooking planks add a delicious smoky flavour to fish, and make the cooking really simple, on or off the barbie

Serves 6 • Ready in 40 mins, plus soaking

1 side of salmon, boneless, skin on
1tbsp light brown sugar
For the salsa:
4 ripe nectarines, stones removed, and roughly chopped
1 red onion, halved and finely sliced
Small handful basil leaves, chopped
Juice 1 lime
You will need:
1 cedar plank (we used Firespice Cedar Planks from Weber, but they're available in major supermarkets)

1 Soak the plank in water for 2 hrs, drain. Put the plank on a hot barbecue grill, with the lid on. Allow to heat and char slightly for around 5 to 10 mins.
2 Set the salmon on the plank, skin side down, season well and sprinkle over the sugar. Replace the lid on the barbecue and cook for 20 to 25 mins. Meanwhile, mix together all the salsa ingredients in a small bowl and serve with the cooked salmon.
TO OVEN COOK
Heat the oven to 180°C/350°F/Gas 4. Heat the soaked, drained plank on an oven tray for 5 mins, then add the salmon and cook, as above.
Per serving: 415 Cals, Fat 22g, Sat fat 4g, Carbs 12g

TIP If you have any leftovers, they will be delicious flaked into a salad

Asian-style BBQ scallops

TIP Use dry white wine as an alternative to mirin but you'll need to add ½tsp of sugar per tbsp.

LOW CALORIE

You can just put these under the grill to cook – it's equally great as a dish for a posh barbecue or dinner party starter

Makes 6 • Ready in 15 mins

½tsp Thai fish sauce
Juice of 1 lime
2½tbsp mirin rice wine
A pinch of dried chilli flakes
6 king scallops in their shell (or you can buy shells from a fishmonger)
20g (¾oz) unsalted butter, cut into small cubes

1 Prepare your barbecue for direct heat. Mix the Thai fish sauce, lime juice, mirin rice wine and dried chilli flakes. Set the king scallops into the shells – or loosen with a knife if they come whole.
2 Divide the mirin mixture between the shells, dot on a little butter and sprinkle over some sea salt. Cook for 3-5 mins or until just cooked through. If you don't want to barbecue the scallops, simply pop them under the grill.
Per serving: Cals 75, Fat 3.5g, Sat fat 2g, Carbs 3g

SUMMER

SIMPLY
Sweet
TREATS

Minimise time in the kitchen and maximise fun in the sun with these brilliantly simple crowd-pleasing puds

We've got you covered with ice cream and iced cheesecake for the ideal summer refreshers

Make the most of the season's best with summer berries at their sweetest

PHOTOGRAPH: GETTY IMAGES

SUMMARY — SUMMER

Chocolate mini cones

TIP Using store-bought custard is a quick ice cream trick giving you more time in the sun!

Chocolate mini cones

After tasting these, you won't want to go back to shop-bought cones

Makes 1l (1¾pt) ice cream and 10 cones
• Ready in 45 mins, plus freezing

For the ice cream:
500ml (17fl oz) tub good-quality vanilla custard
300ml (10fl oz) double cream
300g (10½oz) milk chocolate

For the cones:
2 large egg whites
90g (3oz) icing sugar
3tbsp milk
1tsp vanilla
120g (4½oz) plain flour
30g (1oz) unsalted butter, melted

For the dippings:
100g (3½oz) each milk and white chocolate, melted
5tbsp sesame seeds or finely chopped nuts

1 For the ice cream, pour the custard into a large bowl. Whip the cream until light and fluffy. Melt the chocolate in the microwave until just softened, then stir to melt completely. Fold the cream into the custard, then fold a little of the mixture into the cooled chocolate, add the remainder and mix well. Pour into a container and put in the freezer for 4-5 hrs to set.
2 For the cones, combine the egg whites, icing sugar, milk and vanilla with a pinch of salt. Whisk to combine, add the flour and whisk again until smooth, then stir in the melted butter.
3 Heat a non-stick frying pan to a medium heat (we used a little cooking spray), then pour spoonfuls of the mixture into the pan, in batches, spreading them out with the back of the spoon. Fry for 3-4 mins, until the edges turn caramel in colour. Flip and cook for 1 min on the other side. Remove from the pan and mould into a cone shape, using a tea towel if it's too hot to handle, then leave to cool and set on a wire rack.
4 Once the cones are cool, dip them into the melted chocolate and sprinkle with seeds or chopped nuts (we used black sesame seeds). Keep the cones upside down while the chocolate sets (we put the cones on bottles). Serve scoops of the ice cream in the cones.
Per cone: Cals 534, Fat 37g, Sat fat 21g, Carbs 40g

Iced berry cheesecake

Ice cream meets cheesecake — a match made in pudding heaven

Serves 12 • Ready in 30 mins, plus setting

200g (7oz) shortbread, crushed
75g (3oz) unsalted butter, melted
125g (4½oz) blackcurrants
2tbsp caster sugar
280g (10oz) cream cheese
500g (17½oz) blueberry and vanilla ice cream

For the topping:
200g (7oz) blackcurrants
30g (1oz) caster sugar
2tbsp crème de cassis
4tbsp redcurrant jelly

You will need:
20cm (8in) springform tin, greased and lined with baking paper

1 Blitz the shortbread in a food processor. Melt the butter in a microwave on high for 1 min and pour over the shortbread. Blitz to combine, then press the mixture into the base of the tin.
2 Clean the food processor. Add the blackcurrants and sugar and blend until smooth. Add the cream cheese and ice cream. Blend. Spread over the biscuit base and freeze for at least 1 hr.
3 For the topping, put the blackcurrants in a pan with the sugar and crème de cassis. Heat for a few mins until just softened. Add the redcurrant jelly and warm through until just melted.
4 Remove the cheesecake from the tin and transfer onto a serving plate. Spoon over blackcurrants and syrup.
Per serving: Cals 284, Fat 18g, Sat fat 12g, Carbs 25g

Iced berry cheesecake

TIP Blackcurrants are tricky to find when out of season, however frozen ones will work just as well.

SUMMER

TIP For another fruity favourite, strawberries work fabulously too.

White chocolate popping candy cherries

LOW CAL

Lemon poppy seed layer cake

Filled with blueberry conserve, this showstopper is summer in cake form

Serves 14-16 • Prep 30 mins, plus cooling • Cook 30-35 mins

330g (11½oz) unsalted butter, softened
330g (11½oz) caster sugar, plus 6tbsp
Finely grated zest and juice 3 lemons
6 medium free-range eggs
330g (11½oz) self-raising flour
1tsp baking powder
120g (4¼oz) natural yogurt
100ml (3½fl oz) whole milk
1tsp vanilla bean paste
50g (2½oz) poppy seeds
6tbsp blueberry conserve
Edible flowers, to decorate (optional)

For the mascarpone filling:
500ml (1 pint) double cream
500g (1lb) mascarpone cheese
200g (7oz) icing sugar, sifted
2tsp vanilla bean paste
Finely grated zest 1 lemon

You will need:
2 x 20cm loose bottom cake tins, greased and lined with baking paper

1 1 Heat the oven to 180°C/350°F/Gas 4. Put the butter, caster sugar and lemon zest in a bowl with a pinch of salt, and beat with an electric mixer until fluffy. Add the eggs, one at a time, beating well between each.
2 Sift in the flour and baking powder, and mix until just combined. Fold in the yogurt, milk, vanilla and poppy seeds. Divide the mixture between the tins. Bake for 30-35 mins until risen and golden. Cool in the tins for 10 mins, then turn onto a wire rack and cool completely.
3 Meanwhile, warm the lemon juice and extra 6tbsp caster sugar in a pan until the sugar dissolves. Combine all the filling ingredients in a bowl; whisk to stiff peaks.
4 Cut the cakes to make 4 equal discs. Brush the cut sides with the lemon juice mixture. Put one cake disc on a serving plate; spread with one-fifth of the cream mixture. Top with 2tbsp conserve, then repeat with the remaining cake, filling and conserve. Spread the remaining cream mixture over the top and sides; decorate with edible flowers, if liked.
Per serving (for 16): 751 cals, 55g fat, 34g sat fat, 55g carbs

White chocolate popping candy cherries

For a unique end to a meal that will make your party really pop

Serves 4 • Ready in 15 mins, plus setting

28 cherries on stalks
65g (2½oz) white chocolate
10g (½oz) popping candy

1 Rinse the cherries in cold water and dry really well with a paper towel. Arrange a piece of greaseproof paper on a board or baking tray.
2 Put the white chocolate in a small bowl and place over a small pan of barely simmering water. The bowl should not be touching the water. Carefully melt the chocolate, stirring occasionally until smooth. Remove the bowl from the pan.
3 Holding the cherry stalks, dip just the bottom of the cherries into the melted chocolate and transfer to the greaseproof paper. Sprinkle a tiny pinch of popping candy onto each cherry so that it sticks onto the chocolate. Transfer to the fridge for a few mins, until the chocolate is set.
Per serving: Cals 117, Fat 6g, Sat fat 3g, Carbs 14g

SIMPLY SWEET TREATS

Lemon poppy seed layer cake

SUMMER

Raspberry mousse

A simple dinner party dessert that can be made a day in advance

Serves 8 • Ready in 25 mins, plus chilling

150g (5oz) white chocolate, broken into pieces
2tbsp caster sugar
3 gelatine leaves, soaked in cold water for 5 mins
3 eggs, separated
375ml (12½fl oz) whipping cream
1tsp vanilla extract
2tbsp grenadine or pomegranate cordial
300g (10½oz) raspberries, lightly mashed, plus extra to decorate
Raspberry purée, to serve

1 Melt the chocolate in a bowl set over a pan of barely simmering water. In a separate pan, gently heat the caster sugar with 2tbsp water until it has dissolved, then remove from the heat and stir in the gelatine.
2 Whisk together the egg yolks, cream and vanilla extract until combined. Add the chocolate and the gelatine mix and stir to combine.
3 Stir through the grenadine cordial and the raspberries.
4 Whisk the egg whites until they form stiff peaks, then fold into the rest of the mix until smooth. Spoon into a large bowl and chill for 4 hrs or until set.
5 Top with raspberries and a drizzle of raspberry purée to serve.
Per serving: Cals 344, Fat 27g, Sat fat 16g, Carbs 19g

Raspberry mousse

TIP If you or your guests can't eat raw eggs, swap for 250g (9oz) crème fraîche.

Summer fruit tiramisu

TIP Look out for half bottles of sweet wine to ensure nothing goes to waste!

Summer fruit tiramisu

A fresh twist on the Italian classic

Serves 10 • Ready in 30 mins, plus at least 8 hrs chilling

375g (13oz) mascarpone cheese (or 250g/9oz tub mascarpone cheese and 125g/4½oz cream cheese)
2tbsp golden caster or brown sugar
150ml (5fl oz) double cream
175ml (6fl oz) dessert wine
21 sponge finger biscuits
400g (14oz) strawberries, hulled and sliced if large
150g (5oz) raspberries

For the topping:
150ml (5fl oz) double cream
1tbsp icing sugar
6 strawberries, halved

You will need:
1kg (2lb) loaf tin, lined with cling film, with plenty overhanging

1 Soften the mascarpone with the sugar in a large bowl, then stir in the cream and mix well. Pour the wine into a shallow dish and add 6 sponge fingers for 30 secs, then arrange them on the base of the tin in 3 rows of 2 along the length. Top with half the strawberries and raspberries, then spoon in half the mascarpone mixture and smooth it down.
2 Dip 6 more whole and 3 halves of sponge fingers in wine and arrange in 3 rows down the tin again. Cover with the rest of the fruit, then the rest of the mascarpone. Dip the remaining 7½ fingers in the wine and arrange on top of the mascarpone mixture.
3 Pull the overhanging cling film over the loaf tin and wrap around with more cling film. Put the tin on a baking tray and weigh it down with weights or cans of food. Chill for 8 hrs or overnight.
4 To serve, turn out on to a flat serving platter. Remove the cling film and smooth the sides of the pudding with a palette knife. For the topping, whip the cream with the icing sugar to form soft peaks. Spread it over the top and decorate with strawberries.

Per serving: Cals 386, Fat 32g, Sat fat 21g, Carbs 22g

SUMMER

Strawberry fool trifle

TIP Try this with raspberry jelly, fresh raspberries and chopped peaches for a peach Melba version.

Strawberry fool trifle

Celebrate the season's best with this delightful hybrid pud

Serves 8 • Ready in 40 mins, plus chilling

300g (10½oz) Madeira cake, cut into 2cm (¾in) cubes
4tbsp strawberry or raspberry liqueur
650g (23oz) strawberries, halved or quartered (reserve a few for decoration)
135g (4.8oz) pack strawberry jelly cubes
3tbsp caster sugar
300ml (10fl oz) double cream
150g (5oz) vanilla yoghurt
25g (1oz) mini meringues, broken up
You will need:
1½ litre (2½ pint) trifle bowl

1 Put the Madeira cake cubes into the trifle bowl, drizzle with liqueur and add half the strawberries.
2 Add 360ml (12fl oz) boiling water to the jelly cubes and pour over the cake, then chill until set.
3 Crush the remaining strawberries lightly with the caster sugar. Whip the cream to soft peaks, add the yoghurt and whip again. Fold through the crushed strawberries and spoon onto the jelly. Chill until ready to eat.
4 Just before serving, scatter the mini meringues and the reserved strawberries over the top.
Per serving: Cals 480, Fat 28g, Sat fat 17g, Carbs 41g

Peaches in rosé

LOW CAL

Peaches in rosé

This dainty dessert is best prepared the day before and chilled overnight

Serves 4 • Ready in 20 mins, plus chilling

150ml (5fl oz) rosé
150g (5oz) golden caster sugar
Parings and juice of 1 lemon
1 vanilla pod, split
4 ripe yellow-fleshed peaches
Greek yoghurt, to serve
15g (½oz) pistachios, chopped

1 Pour the rosé and 300ml (10fl oz) water into a small pan, then add the sugar, lemon parings and vanilla. Simmer gently until the sugar dissolves.
2 Carefully add the peaches and poach them gently for 7-10 mins, until they're tender when pierced with a sharp knife.
3 Take the peaches out of the syrup with a slotted spoon and, when cool enough to handle, peel away the skin. Put the peaches back in the poaching liquid and leave to cool completely. Chill.
4 Sieve the syrup. You can serve the peaches in the syrup as it is, or boil it to thicken, and reduce it to about 150ml (5fl oz), adding the lemon juice to taste. Leave to cool.
5 Serve each peach in a puddle of syrupy sauce with a spoonful of thick Greek yoghurt and a sprinkling of chopped pistachios.
Per serving: Cals 231, Fat 2g, Sat fat 0.2g, Carbs 46g

Lemon gin and tonic cheesecake

This dessert is best enjoyed with a refreshing G&T on the side for good measure!

Serves 8 • Ready in 30 mins, plus at least 6 hrs chilling

**200g (7oz) shortbread, crushed
60g (2⅛oz) butter, melted
For the filling:
4 gelatine leaves
Grated juice and zest of 2 lemons
3 x 280g (10oz) packs light soft cheese
100g (3½oz) golden caster sugar
2tbsp gin
2tsp gin and tonic extract (available from Sainsbury's)
150ml (5fl oz) lemon yoghurt
For the topping:
6tbsp lemon curd
1tbsp gin
12 mini lemon meringues
2 lemon slices on cocktail sticks
You will need:
18cm (7in) springform cake tin, greased and lined with baking paper**

1 Mix together the shortbread and butter and press into the base of the tin. Chill while you make the filling.
2 Place the gelatine leaves in a bowl of cold water to soften. Heat the lemon juice in a small pan and bring to the boil. Remove from the heat, squeeze the gelatine leaves in your hand to remove excess water, then add the gelatine to the pan and stir until dissolved. Set aside.
3 Whisk together the soft cheese, lemon zest, sugar, gin, gin and tonic extract, and lemon yoghurt until soft and smooth. Whisk in the lemon juice and gelatine until evenly mixed. Pour into the cake tin, smooth the top and chill for 6 hrs or overnight.
4 To serve, remove the cheesecake from the tin. Mix the lemon curd and gin together and swirl over the top with a spoon. Decorate with mini lemon meringues and lemon slices on cocktail sticks.
Per serving: Cals 519, Fat 26g, Sat fat 16g, Carbs 56g

TIP
Swap the gelatine for agar-agar or other alternatives to make this recipe vegetarian.

SUMMER

Pack a PICNIC

Fill your basket with these tempting treats and head off to the great outdoors…

Picnic sandwich loaf

PACK A PICNIC

Roasted cherry tomato tart

SEASONAL COOKBOOK woman&home 77

SUMMER

Roasted cherry tomato tart

It's worth buying the best cherry tomatoes you can find, as they will make the finished tart taste even better

Serves 6 • Ready in 1 hr, plus chilling and cooling

1 x shortcrust pastry block
For the filling:
500g (1lb) cherry tomatoes
1tbsp olive oil
2tbsp torn basil, plus extra, to garnish
300ml (10fl oz) whipping cream
2 medium eggs
You will also need:
A 23cm (9in) fluted flan tin

1 Set the oven to 190°C/375°F/Gas 5. Put a baking tray inside to heat up.
2 Roll out the pastry to a circle big enough to line the flan tin, then gently lower it in to cover the base and sides. Prick the base and chill for at least 20 mins.
3 Put the tomatoes in a roasting tin and drizzle over the oil. Line the pastry case with baking paper and fill with baking beans. Place the pastry tin on the hot baking tray and put the tin with tomatoes on the shelf below. Cook both for 12 mins. Remove the tomatoes and pastry. Take out the baking paper and beans and return the pastry case to the oven for 5-7 mins until a light golden colour.
4 Reduce the oven temperature to 180°C/350°F/Gas 4. To make the filling, spread the tomatoes out in the pastry case. Scatter over the basil. Beat the cream with the eggs, season, and pour the mixture into the pastry case. Bake in the centre of the oven for 35-40 mins, until the filling is just set. Remove from the oven. Leave to cool for 10 mins before removing from the tin. Scatter more basil leaves on top.
Per serving: Cals 448, Fat 34g, Sat fat 20g, Carbs 24g

Picnic sandwich loaf

This easy filled loaf is much less fiddly than making individual sandwiches and it certainly delivers the wow factor

Serves 6 • Ready in 25 mins

500g (1lb) loaf of crusty round white loaf
3tbsp spicy tomato chutney
150g (5oz) red cabbage, finely sliced
1tbsp half-fat crème fraîche
Squeeze of lemon juice
90g (3oz) pastrami
2 large pickled cucumbers, sliced
100g (3½oz) Emmental cheese slices
2 large organic eggs, hard-boiled, peeled and sliced
30g (1oz) pea shoots

1 Neatly slice a lid off the bread and hollow out the inside, leaving 2cm (¾in) of bread on the crust. Spread the chutney over the inside of the loaf and the cut side of the lid.
2 Mix the red cabbage with the crème fraîche, lemon juice and a pinch of salt, and press into the base. Next, layer up slices of pastrami, cucumber slices, cheese and slices of egg, then top with the pea shoots. Replace the lid and press down the contents.
3 Cut into 6 wedges and wrap it tightly in baking paper tied up with string so it doesn't dismantle during transportation.
Per serving: Cals 359, Fat 10g, Sat fat 5g, Carbs 46g

COOK'S TIP
Whizz the white bread leftovers and freeze as crumbs for coating chicken or fish

Watercress scones

These are also delicious warm from the oven spread with a spicy butter

Serves 8 • Ready in 35-40 mins

200g (7oz) self-raising flour
2 level tsp baking powder
1tsp mustard powder
60g (2½oz) butter
75g (3oz) watercress, finely chopped
75g (3oz) mature Cheddar, grated
150ml (5fl oz) buttermilk or semi-skimmed milk, plus extra for brushing

1 Heat the oven to 220°C/425°F/Gas 7 and line a baking tray with baking paper. Sift the flour, baking powder and mustard into a large bowl and season with salt and pepper. Rub in the butter until the mixture looks like breadcrumbs. Stir in the chopped watercress and about two-thirds of the cheese.
2 Add the milk and mix to a soft dough with a round-bladed knife. Knead lightly on a floured surface and then roll or pat out to a 2½cm (1in) thickness. With a 6cm (2½in) cutter, cut out as many scones as you can, then lightly knead together the trimmings and cut out more scones. Transfer to the lined baking tray. Brush the tops with milk, then sprinkle the rest of the cheese on top.
3 Bake for 20-25 mins in the oven until they are well-risen and golden. Leave to cool. Serve as they are, or split and spread with spicy butter (see tip below).
Per scone (without the spicy butter): Cals 168, Fat 9g, Sat fat 4g, Carbs 20g

COOK'S TIP
For the spicy butter, soften 100g (3½oz) butter, and mix with ¼-½tsp each of ground cumin and coriander, and pinch of smoked paprika

Watercress scones

TIP For something more filling top with smoked salmon and cream cheese.

Middle Eastern couscous with feta

Middle Eastern couscous with feta

Light and refreshing, this new take on Greek salad goes well with pastry-based dishes, such as the tomato tart and sharing sausage roll

Serves 4 • Ready in 25 mins

200g (7oz) giant couscous
2tbsp each chopped fresh parsley and mint
6tbsp French dressing
Juice ½ lemon
400g (14oz) can chickpeas, rinsed and drained
¾ cucumber, chopped
2 tomatoes, chopped
2 cooked beetroot, chopped
6 radishes, chopped
100g (3½oz) feta cheese, broken into pieces
4tbsp pomegranate seeds
2tbsp olive oil
Mint leaves, to garnish

1 Cook the couscous in boiling water for 6-8 mins until tender. Drain, rinse under cold water and drain again.
2 Tip the couscous into a large bowl, add the chopped parsley and mint, French dressing, lemon juice and chickpeas and stir to mix.
3 Scatter the cucumber, tomatoes, beetroot, radishes, feta and pomegranate seeds over the top. Drizzle over the olive oil, season with freshly ground black pepper and top with mint leaves.
Per serving: Cals 230, Fat 10g, Sat fat 2g, Carbs 26g

COOK'S TIP
Make this vegan-friendly by buying a feta alternative such as Violife

Broad bean hummus

TIP Turn this snack into a light lunch by adding lightly toasted flatbreads and feta.

This is creamy, delicious, and looks so fresh and vibrant!

Serves 4 • Ready in 20 mins

450g (1lb) podded broad beans
2 garlic cloves
12 mint leaves
1tbsp lemon juice
1tbsp tahini
4tbsp olive oil
2tsp toasted sesame seeds

1 Boil a pan of water, add beans and garlic, then simmer for 5 mins; drain.
2 Put the beans and garlic in a food processor with a pinch of salt. Add the mint leaves, lemon juice and tahini. Blitz to combine. Gradually add 3tbsp olive oil and blend until smooth.
3 Spoon into a serving bowl. Just before serving, drizzle with 1tbsp olive oil and sprinkle with sesame seeds.
Per serving: Cals 242, Fat 19.5g, Sat fat 3g, Carbs 8.5g

SUMMER

Spicy vegetable samosas

Baking instead of frying makes these little bites healthier

Makes 12 • Ready in 1 hr 15 mins

600g (21oz) vegetables, such as peppers, aubergine, sweet potatoes, courgettes
1-2tbsp curry paste
6tbsp chopped fresh coriander
270g (9½oz) pack filo pastry, 6 sheets (we used Jus-Rol)
75g (3oz) butter, melted
Paprika, optional
You will also need:
A baking tray lined with greaseproof paper

1 Heat the oven to 200°C/400°F/Gas 6. Cut the vegetables into chunks and put into a large roasting tin. Drizzle with olive oil, season with salt and pepper, and roast for 30 mins. Allow to cool a little before making the filling.
2 Chop the vegetables more finely (or whizz them with a stick blender), stir in the curry paste and coriander. Check the seasoning according to your taste.
3 Keep the filo sheets under a damp clean tea towel as you assemble the samosas. Brush 1 sheet of pastry at a time with a little melted butter, cut the sheet in half lengthways, and then put 2tbsp of filling at the bottom of each strip. Fold over, and keep folding over on itself to create little triangles. Place them on the lined baking tray and brush with butter. Repeat to use up all the pastry and filling. Sprinkle with some paprika, if you like. Bake in the oven for 25-30 mins, or until they are golden.
Per serving: Cals 140, Fat 6g, Sat fat 3g, Carbs 17g

Sharing Tex-Mex sausage roll

This is great served hot or cold as an alfresco main course in the garden

Serves 6-8 • Ready in 55 mins

400g (14oz) pack sausages, skinned
75g (3oz) dried white breadcrumbs
1 small onion, finely chopped
1-2 green chillies, deseeded and chopped
1tbsp chipotle paste
2-3tbsp freshly chopped coriander
400g (14oz) can kidney beans, drained and rinsed
320g (11oz) pack ready-rolled puff pastry
1 egg, beaten, to glaze
You will also need:
A baking tray, lined with baking paper

1 Heat the oven to 200°C/400°F/Gas 6. Tip sausage meat into a bowl and add the breadcrumbs, onion, chillies, chipotle paste and coriander. Season with salt and pepper and mix well. Add the kidney beans and mix them in, taking care not to break them down too much.
2 Unroll the pastry sheet and cut it lengthways, not quite in half, so that one section is wider than the other.
3 Place the narrower piece of pastry on the lined baking tray and brush all around the edge with water. Place the sausage-meat filling on top, pressing it to give a smooth, even shape, leaving a small rim of uncovered pastry all the way round the edge.
4 Take the other pastry sheet and fold it loosely in half. Make lots of cuts, about 1cm (½in) apart, all down the folded edge, leaving a slightly wider section at either end. Open the pastry out and place it over the filling. Press the edges down. Trim them and make small cuts into the edge with a knife to create a pattern.
5 Brush the pastry with the beaten egg, to glaze. Bake the sausage roll for 30-40 mins, or until the pastry is golden. Remove it from the oven and slide on to a wire rack. Allow to cool, before transporting it in a plastic container.
Per serving (for 6): Cals 544, Fat 33g, Sat fat 14g, Carbs 36g

PACK A PICNIC

TIP
Serve the spicy sausage roll hot or cold with a chunky salsa to dip it into.

Sharing Tex-Mex sausage roll

AUTUMN

Autumn

- 88 Roasted pumpkin and blue cheese lasagna
- 88 Pesto roasted squash
- 89 Pumpkin pecan pie
- 92 Slow roasted Provençale lamb
- 92 Best beef chilli
- 96 Crispy duck cassoulet
- 96 Pork and cider casserole
- 96 Fennel sausage parpadelle
- 98 Mushroom, chestnut and greens pie
- 99 Sausage and butternut squash stew
- 100 Sweet miso pork
- 100 Thai red chicken curry
- 101 Sausage hotpot with cheesy garlic bread
- 103 Creamy squash and sage penne
- 103 Brined chicken with pumpkin, pears and cider
- 106 Fig tarte tatin
- 107 Blueberry and apple cobbler
- 110 Chocolate cherry roly-poly
- 110 Chocolate and amaretto bread and butter pudding
- 110 Plum and hazelnut Bakewell tart
- 112 Caramelised pear and blackberry crumble
- 112 Rustic plum pie
- 114 Chocolate banoffee sparkler cake
- 115 Toffee apples with a twist
- 115 Cobweb chocolate tart
- 117 Toffee apple tart
- 117 Pulled pork baps
- 117 Quorn chilli pitta pockets

AUTUMN

AUTUMN

What's in SEASON

Autumn sees the arrival of comforting root vegetables we associate with the colder months. It's also the time for rich game meat, including grouse and venison

✢ APPLES
Over 7,000 apple varieties are in existence, but we only use around 12 of them in Britain. Find new types at your nearest farmers' market.

✢ BEETROOT
The earthy flavours of beetroot pair really well with dairy and cheeses.

✢ BLACKBERRIES
These hedgerow favourites provide delicious snacking on country walks, and are perfect packed into a pie!

✢ CABBAGE
Whatever the variety, make sure it's bright with crisp leaves. Try stir-frying green cabbage with chilli, garlic and soy for an easy Asian-inspired side.

✢ CAULIFLOWER
Roasted cauliflower makes a great addition to salads. Blitz it to make a low-carb rice alternative. Bake a whole head of cauliflower in a rich tomato ragu for a hearty veggie main.

✢ CAVOLO NERO
These delicious dark green leaves are packed with nutrition — we love them pan-fried with a little butter or olive oil and a squeeze of lemon.

✢ CELERIAC
This peculiar-looking root has a subtle and nutty flavour. Use it to make a mash, a rich and creamy gratin, or even for healthier chunky chips.

✢ FENNEL
A favourite for gratins or simply roasting until caramelised in delicious olive oil. You'll either love or hate it!

✢ LEEKS
Steamed, roasted or fried (ideally in butter), they are simply delicious!

✢ MUSHROOMS
Wild mushroom season is upon us — but if you're not an expert, stick to buying from supermarkets or grocers to avoid any dangerous varieties.

✢ QUINCE
British quinces are available until December — the high level of pectin makes them perfect for jams.

✢ RADICCHIO
This Italian lettuce variety is packed full of nutrition. Grilling or sautéing will bring out all the sweet flavours.

✢ SLOES
Sloe gin is so on trend — and you can forage for sloe berries yourself, just beware of the nasty thorns.

✢ SWEDE
Not just for Burns Night, this delicious member of the cabbage family bulks up any soup or stew.

✢ SWISS CHARD
Who can resist the lovely bright colours of these stalks?

✢ TOMATO
Autumn is the last stretch for seasonal tomatoes in the UK as they are harvested from June to October — try our favourites from the Isle of Wight!

✢ TURNIP
An underutilised vegetable, try roasting with a little butter and lemon zest.

✢ CRAB
This delicious crustacean comes into season in April and is widely available until November.

✢ DUCK
Easier to prepare than you think: pan-fry or roast and serve with greens.

✢ GROUSE
Still with us for the short season, grouse are delicious roasted — one per person, so the maths is easy!

✢ VENISON
Wild venison season starts 21 October and lasts until 15 February. Delicious with bacon; just don't overcook it

PUMPKINS & SQUASH

✧ These gorgeous vegetables are perfectly in season at this time of year so embrace seasonality with the warming dishes on the next page.

✧ We have something for everyone, from a midweek dinner to a recipe perfect for sharing at a dinner party.

✧ Don't just use pumpkins for carving – these dishes will inspire you to rethink what you make with them.

SEASONAL COOKBOOK woman&home 87

AUTUMN

TIP Not a fan of blue cheese? Goat's cheese would also be delicious here.

Roasted pumpkin and blue cheese lasagne

Roasted pumpkin and blue cheese lasagne

This is a truly warming dish for colder days

Serves 6 • Ready in 1 hr 15 mins

1 small pumpkin or 2 butternut squash, peeled, cut in thick slices
3tbsp olive oil
A small bunch of fresh sage
200g (7oz) fresh lasagne sheets
2 x 400g (14oz) cans cherry tomatoes, drained
300g (10½oz) Blacksticks Blue cheese or Cropwell Bishop Blue Shropshire, crumbled

For the béchamel sauce:
40g (1½oz) butter
40g (1½oz) plain flour
500ml (17fl oz) semi-skimmed milk

1 Heat the oven to 190°C/375°F/Gas 7. Toss the pumpkin in the oil and put into a roasting tin. Add a few sprigs of sage and season. Roast for 30 mins.
2 For the béchamel, melt the butter in a pan, stir in the plain flour and cook for a few mins. Whisk in the milk and stir until thickened. Meanwhile, chop the remaining sage.
3 Put a little sauce in the base of a serving dish, then a layer of pasta, sauce, pumpkin, tomatoes, cheese and sage. End with a layer of pumpkin, sage and cheese. Bake for 20-30 mins. Serve with green salad and some crusty bread.
Per serving: Cals 504, Fat 28g, Sat fat 12g, Carbs 37g

Pesto roasted squash

This would make a great centrepiece for a dinner party

Serves 4 • Ready in 1 hr 30 mins

2 medium (about 1kg/2lb) butternut squash
4tbsp fresh green pesto
1 onion, peeled and cut into chunks
1tbsp olive oil
250g (9oz) cherry tomatoes
4 rashers streaky bacon, chopped
80g (3oz) baby-leaf spinach
80g (3oz) feta cheese, crumbled
35g (1oz) sun-blush tomatoes, drained and chopped
2tbsp pine nuts, toasted

1 Heat the oven to 200°C/400°F/Gas 6. Cut the butternut squash in half, scoop out the seeds and cut crosses into the flesh. Brush with ½ the pesto and season. Cover with greased foil and bake for 1 hr or until tender.
2 Put the onion in a roasting tin with the olive oil and cook for 25 mins. Add the cherry tomatoes and streaky bacon, and cook for 20 mins. Stir in the spinach, remaining pesto, feta and sun-blush tomatoes, season and set aside.
3 Remove the butternut squash from the oven. Scoop out a little of the flesh and mix with the veg filling. Spoon into the holes in the squash and cook for 10 mins. Sprinkle over the pine nuts.
Per serving: Cals 417, Fat 27g, Sat fat 6g, Carbs 27g

Pesto roasted squash

88 woman&home SEASONAL COOKBOOK

Pumpkin pecan pie

A true autumn classic, this is the perfect way to finish a seasonal feast in style

Serves 8 • Ready in 2 hr 30 mins, plus chilling

225g (8oz) ready-made shortcrust pastry

For the filling:
450g (1lb) pumpkin, halved and deseeded
2 egg yolks
60g (2½oz) light muscovado sugar
125ml (4fl oz) double cream
2tbsp maple syrup
½tsp each ground cinnamon and Grated nutmeg
½tsp vanilla extract

For the topping:
6 tbsp maple syrup
75g (3oz) salted pecan halves
1tbsp icing sugar, for dusting (optional)

You will need:
20cm (8in) fluted tart tin
Greased baking paper
Baking beans

1 Set the oven to 200°C/400°F/Gas 6. Put the pumpkin into a roasting tin. Roast for 40 mins until the flesh is tender.
2 Line the tin with the pastry. Chill for 15 mins and then trim off the edges. Fill the pastry with the baking paper and baking beans. Bake for 15 mins then remove the paper and beans. Cook for 5 more mins until pastry is golden.
3 Reduce the oven temperature to 160°C/320°F/Gas 3.
4 For the filling, scoop out the pumpkin flesh into a large bowl and use a potato masher to mash it until smooth.
5 Put egg yolks in a bowl with sugar and whisk until foamy. Whisk in the cream, maple syrup, spices and vanilla extract. Whisk this mixture into the pumpkin.
6 Spoon the filling into the pastry case and bake for 1 hr until the filling is firm.
7 For the topping, put the maple syrup into a pan with pecans. Warm through, then arrange pecans on pie. Pour syrup over and return to oven for 10 mins.
8 Take the pie out of the oven, leave to cool, and chill. Dust with icing sugar, if liked.

Per serving: Cals 365, Fat 25g, Sat fat 9g, Carbs 32g

AUTUMN

Feeding a CROWD

These dishes are perfect for when you get in from the cold and need to warm up fast!

Many of these delicious autumnal warmers can be prepared ahead of time for stress-free entertaining

Feeding vegetarians? Treat them to our showstopper mushroom, chestnut and greens pie

FEEDING A CROWD

Slow roasted provençale lamb

DAIRY FREE
GLUTEN FREE

Slow roasted provençale lamb

Tender, delicious, slow-cooked meat — best with French beans and roast potatoes

Serves 6 • Ready in 2 hrs 30 mins

1¼kg (2lb 12oz) half a leg or shoulder of lamb
4 garlic cloves, sliced
A few rosemary stalks
3tbsp balsamic vinegar
2tsp all-purpose seasoning
2 onions, sliced
2 large heads of fennel, sliced
4 tbsp olive oil
400g (14oz) midi plum tomatoes
100g (3½oz) Kalamata olives
A few parsley leaves

1 Heat oven to 180°C/350°F/Gas 4. Slash the lamb in several places and push in 2 of the garlic cloves and rosemary leaves. Drizzle over the vinegar. Season and sprinkle over all-purpose seasoning.
2 Put the lamb in a roasting tin or a large flameproof casserole dish with the onion and fennel. Add 4tbsp water. Drizzle over the olive oil, cover and roast in the oven for 2 hrs.
3 Add the tomatoes and the olives and cook uncovered in the oven for 20 mins or until the meat and vegetables are tender. Sprinkle with the parsley to serve.
Per serving: Cals 375, Fat 23g, Sat fat 7g, Carbs 6g

TIP Leaving the meat to rest after cooking will make it extra tender and succulent.

Best beef chilli

A classic winter warmer, serve with rice or with baked potatoes for a hearty meal

Serves 8 • Ready in 3 hrs

1kg (2lb) beef brisket, cut into small chunks
4tbsp oil
2 red onions, peeled and diced
3 sticks of celery, chopped
4 cloves garlic, peeled and crushed
3 red chillies, deseeded and finely sliced
2tbsp cumin
2tsp smoked paprika
2 x 400g (14oz) tin finely chopped tomatoes
1tbsp tomato purée
500ml (17fl oz) beef stock
2tbsp brown sugar
2tbsp sherry vinegar
1 x 400g (14oz) kidney beans
Coriander, to serve
Sour cream, to serve

1 Heat the oven to 150°C/300°F/Gas 2. In a large ovenproof casserole dish, fry the steak in ½ the oil in batches until evenly browned on all sides then remove with a slotted spoon and set aside. Add the remaining oil to the casserole and fry the onions and celery, covered but occasionally stirring, for 10-15 mins until soft.
2 Add the garlic, chillies, cumin and paprika and cook for a further 2 mins until fragrant. Return the meat to the pan along with the tinned tomatoes, tomato puree, beef stock, sugar and sherry vinegar. Cover and put in the oven to cook for 2 hrs 30 mins or until the meat is tender.
3 Add the beans for the final 30 mins of cooking to heat through and season to taste. Serve the chilli with fluffy rice, coriander and soured cream or in warm tortilla wraps.
Per serving: Cals 300, Fat 11g, Sat fat 3g, Carbs 15g

Best beef chilli

TIP
This makes for a chilli with a real kick – if you prefer yours mild, skimp on the chillies.

AUTUMN

DAIRY FREE

Crispy duck cassoulet

Pork and cider casserole

TIP When adapting recipes for a slow cooker, use less liquid as it doesn't evaporate.

AUTUMN

Crispy duck cassoulet

For a little extra indulgence, serve with chunks of freshly baked, crusty bread to mop up all the juices with

Serves 6 • Ready in 1 hr 45 mins

200g (7oz) smoked lardons
300g (10½oz) sausage, sliced
2tbsp duck fat or olive oil
2 shallots, finely diced
1 stick celery, diced
1 carrot, diced
1 bouquet garni
2 garlic cloves, crushed
400g (14oz) dried haricot beans, soaked overnight
6 confit duck legs
Crusty bread, to serve

1 Heat the oven to 180°C/350°F/Gas 4. In a large casserole dish, fry the lardons for 5 mins, until browned. Add the sausage and fry for a couple more mins. Add the duck fat, shallots, celery, carrot, bouquet garni and garlic. Fry for a couple more mins until slightly softened. Add the beans, along with 2l (3½pt) water. Put in the oven, uncovered, and cook for 1 hr 30 mins, until everything is soft. Check halfway through and add more water if needed.
2 Meanwhile, cook the confit duck legs according to the pack instructions. Serve the duck on top of the cassoulet, with bread on the side.
Per serving: Cals 793, Fat 38g, Sat fat 13g, Carbs 34g

> **TIP** This freezes really well – just make sure everything is completely cold before transferring to the freezer

Pork and cider casserole

A stress-free meal perfect for sharing with friends

Serves 4 • Ready in 4 hrs 20 mins (slow cooked)/1 hr 50 mins

2tbsp olive oil
600g (21oz) pork loin fillet, sliced
1 red onion, thinly sliced
2 garlic cloves, grated
2tsp fennel seeds
350ml-500ml (12-17fl oz) dry cider
Zest and juice of 2 lemons
3tbsp crème fraîche
75g (3oz) green olives
3tbsp capers
Handful flat-leaf parsley, chopped

1 Heat a slow cooker to high or the oven to 160°C/320°F/Gas 3. Heat ½ the oil in a large frying pan. Add the pork, in batches, and fry for 2 mins on each side until browned. Transfer to the slow cooker or a casserole dish.
2 Heat the remaining oil in the pan, add the onion, garlic and fennel seeds and cook for 5 mins. Add 350ml (12fl oz) cider (500ml/17fl oz if using the oven), bring to the boil and pour over the pork. Scatter over most of the lemon zest and all of the lemon juice, cover and cook for 4 hrs in the slow cooker (1½ hrs in oven).
3 Stir through the crème fraîche. Season and scatter over the remaining ingredients to serve.
Per serving: Cals 575, Fat 32g, Sat fat 13.2g, Carbs 10.8g

Fennel sausage pappardelle

We've used fresh pappardelle, which is easy to find at your local supermarket, but tagliatelle (pappardelle's skinnier sister) will work well too

Serves 6 • Ready in 30 mins

400g (14oz) free-range pork and fennel sausages
2tsp fennel seeds, bashed in a pestle and mortar
1tsp chilli flakes
1 large fennel bulb, cut into wedges
2tbsp olive oil plus extra for drizzling
1 onion, peeled and diced
2 garlic cloves, crushed
3 rosemary sprigs, finely chopped
450g (1lb) fresh pappardelle or tagliatelle
150ml (5fl oz) white wine
Zest of 1 lemon
45g (1½oz) Parmesan cheese, grated

1 Squeeze the meat from the sausages into a bowl with the fennel seeds and chilli flakes.
2 Reserve extra fennel leaves for garnish. Heat the olive oil in a large, deep frying pan over a medium-high heat, fry the fennel for a few minutes until coloured. Add the sausage meat and onion, stirring often, and cook for 10 mins, until the meat is browned. Add the crushed garlic and rosemary and cook for another min. Cook the pappardelle according to packet instructions.
3 Add the white wine to the meat mixture and allow to reduce for a few mins. Finely grate over the zest of 1 lemon and then turn down to heat. Toss through the cooked, drained pappardelle. Divide between your bowls and finish with a grating of Parmesan, a drizzle of olive oil and the reserved fennel leaves.
Per serving: Cals 500, Fat 24g, Sat fat 6g, Carbs 44g

FEEDING A CROWD

TIP
The quality of your sausages is what makes or breaks this dish, so make sure to choose your absolute favourites!

Fennel sausage pappardelle

SEASONAL COOKBOOK woman&home

Mushroom, chestnut and greens pie

GREAT FOR VEGGIES

Mushroom, chestnut and greens pie

A perfect autumnal vegetarian treat, this is a real showstopper

Serves 6 • Ready in 1 hr 45 mins, plus chilling

500g (1lb) shortcrust pastry
15g (1tbsp) dried porcini mushrooms
1tbsp rapeseed oil
1 large onion, chopped
2 sprigs of thyme
2 leeks, sliced
3 garlic cloves, crushed
800g (1lb 12oz) mixed mushrooms – we used chestnut, girolles, closed cup and chanterelles, roughly chopped
200g (7oz) bunch spring greens, trimmed and sliced
180g (6oz) pack cooked and peeled chestnuts, roughly chopped
1½tbsp polenta
1 small egg, beaten

You will need:
2kg (4½lb) loaf tin, greased

1 Cut two sheets of foil, one long enough to line the length of the loaf tin and the other to line the width, both with some overhang. Fold each over to make thick strips about 5cm (2in) wide. Set them into the tin to make a cross, to help lift out the pie.
2 Roll the pastry out to about 1cm (½in) thick and line the tin, leaving a little excess pastry over the sides. Cut out extra strips about 2cm (¾in) to go around the edge. Cut out a rectangle of pastry for the lid, about 4cm (1½in) wider than the top of the tin, and with any excess pastry, cut into leaves to decorate. Chill for 30 mins. Heat the oven to 200°C/400°F/Gas 6. Line the pastry with foil and fill with baking beans; blind bake for 15 mins. Remove the beans and cook for another 15 mins.
3 Soak the porcini mushrooms in enough boiling water to just cover them; set aside. Heat the oil in a large frying pan and cook the onion for 5 mins over a medium heat. Add the thyme, leeks and garlic. Cook for 5 more mins, set aside. In the same pan, cook the mixed mushrooms for 5 mins, or until softened. Put in a colander set over the sink for 10 mins, so all the excess moisture drains off. Set the greens in a bowl and cover with boiling water for 4 mins, drain and rinse under water. Drain and chop the porcini mushrooms.
4 In a large bowl, mix the greens, all the mushrooms, the leek mixture and chestnuts. Season well. Sprinkle the polenta in the base of the pastry case and then spoon in the filling. Brush the sides with egg and stick the pastry strips around the edges, brush these with egg and add the pastry lid and pierce 2 holes in the middle of it. Pinch around the edges to seal. Stick on pastry leaves and glaze with egg. Chill for 30 mins (freeze at this stage, cook at the same oven temperature for 50-60 mins from frozen). Bake for 30 mins.
Per serving: Cals 532, Fat 30g, Sat fat 10g, Carbs 48g

> **TIP** Draining off the excess moisture will help to prevent soggy pastry

FEEDING A CROWD

Sausage and butternut squash stew

Sausage and butternut squash stew

Eating well doesn't have to mean going hungry – fill up with this good-for-you stew!

Serves 4 • Ready in 1 hr

8 lean pork sausages
350g (12oz) butternut squash, deseeded, peeled and cut into chunks
1 red onion, cut into wedges
395g (14oz) can cherry tomatoes
100ml (3½fl oz) balsamic vinegar
400g (14oz) can cannellini beans, drained
2 rosemary sprigs

1 Heat the oven to 200°C/400°F/Gas 6. Put the pork sausages, butternut squash and red onion in a roasting tin and roast for 30 mins.

2 Take the tin out and turn the sausages and vegetables. Add the cherry tomatoes, balsamic vinegar, cannellini beans and rosemary sprigs.

3 Return to the oven for a further 15 mins.

Per serving: Cals 305, Fat 4g, Sat fat 1.5g, Carbs 34g

TIP Buying a whole squash and peeling it is a little more effort but much cheaper than buying prepared!

DAIRY FREE
LOW CALORIE

Sweet miso pork

Sweet miso pork

TIP Any leftovers would be delicious in a crunchy Asian salad.

DAIRY FREE

What's not to love about slow-cooked pork? This is glazed with a miso-based paste that makes it sweet, sour and sticky all at once!

Serves 6 • Ready in 6 hrs 30 mins

1¼-1½kg (2.6-3.3lb) pork shoulder, boned and rolled, skin scored

For the glaze:
250g (9oz) pack sweet white miso paste
50ml (3½ tbsp) soy sauce
100g (5 tbsp) runny honey
75ml (5 tbsp) mirin (Japanese rice wine)

1 To make the glaze, mix all the ingredients together in a bowl until well combined. This will make more than you need but it keeps for ages in the fridge and is great with chicken, fish or added to vegetables as a stir-fry sauce.

2 Heat the oven to 130°C/266°F/Gas ½. Set the pork on a rack over a roasting tin (it's a good idea to line it with foil) and brush the meat only, not the skin, with 1-2tbsp of glaze. Cook slowly, covered loosely with foil, for 6 hrs, until super tender. Glaze the meat every hour or so.

3 When you are ready to serve, turn the oven up to 200°C/400°F/Gas 6. Blast the pork until it starts to crackle, then brush the crackling and the meat with a little glaze before serving. Delicious with mash or rice and try some cavolo nero or greens stir-fried in the miso glaze.
Per serving: Cals 541, Fat 28g, Sat fat 9g, Carbs 23g

Thai red chicken curry

If you can't find Thai shallots, European ones will do

Serves 8 • Ready in 40 mins

3tbsp rapeseed or vegetable oil
8 Thai shallots, peeled and sliced
8 chicken breasts, skin removed and cut into strips
4tbsp Thai red curry paste
2 x 400ml (13½fl oz) cans coconut milk
300ml (10fl oz) chicken stock
3tbsp Thai fish sauce
1tbsp caster sugar
2 red peppers, deseeded and sliced
200g (7oz) baby spinach leaves
Juice of 1 lime, plus wedges to serve
1 bunch basil, leaves torn
1 bunch coriander, chopped

1 Heat the oil in a deep frying pan and fry the shallots for a few mins. Add the chicken and fry for 5 mins.
2 Stir in the curry paste and cook for 1 min, then add the coconut milk, stock, fish sauce and sugar. Stir. Add the peppers and simmer for 15 mins.
3 Add the spinach, lime juice, basil leaves and coriander, cook for 1 min, then turn off the heat and serve with rice and the lime wedges.
Per serving: Cals 435, Fat 25g, Sat fat 16g, Carbs 10g

Thai red chicken curry

100 woman&home SEASONAL COOKBOOK

Sausage hotpot with cheesy garlic bread

TIP It pays to invest in a large, good quality casserole dish – and make sure it's flameproof.

Sausage hotpot with cheesy garlic bread

Simply oozing with spicy flavours, you'll be wanting to make this lovely dish time and again

Serves 6 • Ready in 45 mins

225g (8oz) chorizo, thickly sliced
12 good-quality sausages, sliced
1 red onion, sliced
1 yellow and 1 red pepper, sliced
Large pinch of dried oregano
200ml (7fl oz) white wine
500ml (17fl oz) passata
100ml (3½fl oz) vegetable stock
1 bay leaf
260g (9oz) pack frozen garlic bread
50g (2oz) Cheddar, grated
1tbsp chopped parsley, to serve

1 Heat the oven to 180°C/350°F/Gas 4. Heat a large casserole dish, add the chorizo and fry until it starts to colour, then turn and cook on the other side. Remove with a slotted spoon and add the sausages. Brown all over on a medium heat, then remove to join the chorizo.
2 If the pan is a little dry, add a splash of oil and cook the onion, peppers and oregano for 10 mins. Slice the sausages and return to the pan with the chorizo and wine. Allow to bubble for 2-3 mins.
3 Stir in the passata, stock and bay leaf, and season. Bring to the boil. Arrange the garlic bread on top, add the cheese, then bake for 30 mins. Sprinkle with parsley and serve with buttered green veg.
Per serving: Cals 690, Fat 45g, Sat fat 16g, Carbs 36g

AUTUMN

Creamy squash and sage penne

Creamy squash and sage penne

This squash and sage dish warms up any cool evenings, not only for its colours but its hearty flavours

Serves 4 • Ready in 1 hr 20 mins

1 medium butternut squash, peeled, deseeded and cut into small chunks
3tbsp olive oil
1 small bunch of fresh sage leaves
75g (2½oz) roughly chopped hazelnuts or walnuts
350g (12oz) penne
2 banana shallots, peeled and finely sliced
1tsp thyme leaves
5tbsp cream
50g (2oz) Parmesan, grated

1 Heat the oven to 200°C/400°F/Gas 6. Toss the squash with 2tbsp of the olive oil in a large baking tray and season. Roast for around 40-50 mins, or until soft and tender. Add the sage leaves and hazelnuts for the last 5 mins. Cook the pasta according to packet instructions.
2 In a large saucepan fry the shallots with thyme leaves in remaining olive oil, on a medium heat.
3 When the pasta is al dente, drain and add to the fried onion, along with the cooked butternut squash (reserve the sage leaves for topping). Stir to mix, then add the cream and Parmesan. Divide between bowls and serve with the crispy sage on top.
Per serving: Cals 700, Fat 29g, Sat fat 7g, Carbs 38g

TIP Crispy breadcrumbs would also be lovely sprinkled on top for crunch

Brined chicken with pumpkin, pears and cider

TIP For the best result, buy the highest quality free range or organic chicken you can.

The brining process will keep the chicken in this dish beautifully moist

Serves 4-6 • Ready in 1 hr 30 mins, plus brining and resting time

200ml (7fl oz) dry cider
100g (3½oz) demerara sugar
2tbsp rock salt
1tbsp black peppercorns
2 thyme sprigs
3 bay leaves, crushed
1 large chicken
10 shallots, halved
4 bay leaves
5 thyme sprigs, plus extra leaves to serve
50g (2oz) butter, softened
1 small pumpkin or round squash, deseeded and cut into wedges
3 pears, halved and cored
2tbsp olive oil
150ml (5fl oz) dry cider

1 Mix the first 6 ingredients with 200ml (6½fl oz) water. Put the chicken in a zip-seal bag and pour in the brine. Seal, place in a dish and chill for 6-24 hrs, turning the bag occasionally.
2 Heat the oven to 190°C/375°F/Gas 5. Remove the chicken from the brine, rinse in cool water and pat dry. Put 4 shallot halves, a bay leaf and a thyme sprig inside its body cavity. Loosen the skin from the breast and put a knob of butter and the remaining bay leaves between the breast and skin.
3 Spread the remaining butter over the bird's legs and breast. Put the chicken in an ovenproof dish, cover loosely with foil and roast for 20 mins.
4 Uncover the chicken and add the remaining shallots and thyme, and the pumpkin and pears to the tin. Drizzle over the olive oil, season and pour in the dry cider. Reduce the heat to 180°C/350°F/Gas 4 and roast for about 50 mins, or until the juices run clear when a skewer is inserted into the thigh.
5 Transfer the chicken to a board, cover with foil and allow to rest for 10 mins. Garnish with thyme leaves, then carve.
Per serving: Cals 756-504, Fat 29-19g, Sat fat 11-7g, Carbs 45-30g

SEASONAL COOKBOOK **woman&home** 103

AUTUMN

Warming PUDS

Celebrate gorgeous seasonal fruits such as apples, pears, plums, blackberries and figs in comforting cobblers, crumbles and tarts

Indulge in retro favourites such as jam roly-poly and bread and butter pudding brought bang up to date with simple flavour twists

WARMING PUDS

SEASONAL COOKBOOK woman&home 105

AUTUMN

Fig tarte tatin

Fig tarte tatin

A delicious new take on a classic

Serves 6 • Ready in 50 mins, plus cooling

60g (2½oz) caster sugar
60g (2½oz) butter
½tsp vanilla extract
8 figs, stalks trimmed, halved
320g (11oz) ready-rolled puff pastry
Greek yoghurt, to serve

You will need:
20cm (8in) ovenproof frying pan or cake tin (not loose-based)

1 Heat the oven to 220°C/425°F/Gas 7. Gently heat the sugar in the pan until it dissolves and turns a golden brown. Stir in the butter and vanilla.
2 Put the figs into the pan on top of the caramel, cut-side down, in a single layer to fit snugly. If using a cake tin, pour the caramel into the tin and arrange the figs on top.
3 Cut out a circle of pastry from the sheet, a little larger than the pan or tin. Drape it over the figs and tuck the sides down to enclose the fruit. Prick the pastry with a fork and bake in the oven for 25 mins until the pastry is risen and golden.
4 Remove from the oven and allow to cool for 5-10 mins. Run a sharp knife around the edge of the pastry, put a serving pan on the top of the pan or tin and turn the tart out. Serve with Greek yoghurt on the side.
Per serving: Cals 343, Fat 21g, Sat fat 12g, Carbs 33g

TIP For a gluten-free tart, switch to a pack of Jus-rol Ready-rolled Gluten-free Puff Pastry, (Waitrose, Ocado and Tesco).

DIVINE DESSERTS

Blueberry and apple cobbler

An American twist on a fruit crumble with juicy blueberries and a buttermilk scone topping

Serves 5 • Ready in 55 mins

500g (1lb) blueberries
2 apples, peeled, cored and sliced
60g (2½oz) golden caster sugar
1tbsp thickening granules
½tsp ground mixed spice
For the cobbler:
150g (5oz) self-raising flour
60g (2½oz) butter, chilled
100g (3½oz) golden caster sugar
100ml (3½fl oz) buttermilk
1tbsp golden granulated sugar
You will need:
1¼l (2pt) buttered ovenproof dish

1 Heat the oven to 200°C/400°F/Gas 6. Put the blueberries and prepared apples into the buttered ovenproof dish. Sprinkle with the sugar, thickening granules and mixed spice.
2 To make the cobbler, put the flour into a food processor with small chunks of butter and then gently pulse for a few seconds until it forms crumbs. Add the golden caster sugar and buttermilk and blend briefly to form a soft dough.
3 Pull off pieces of the dough and arrange on top of the fruit, but don't cover it completely. Sprinkle with a little granulated sugar and bake for 35-40 mins until the fruit is tender and bubbling and the topping is well risen and golden. Serve in small dishes or cups.
Per serving: Cals 331, Fat 9g, Sat fat 5g, Carbs 60g

TIP
Use the cobbler recipe to make buttermilk scones – shape and bake for 10 mins at 210°C/410°F/Gas 7.

Blueberry and apple cobbler

SEASONAL COOKBOOK **woman&home** 107

AUTUMN

Chocolate cherry roly-poly

TIP
If you can't get black cherries in kirsch, use canned or frozen cherries and let them steep for 1 hr in a few tbsp of kirsch or cherry brandy.

DIVINE DESSERTS

Chocolate and amaretto bread and butter pudding

TIP
Using slightly stale bread is best so it soaks up all the chocolatey custard, but if you've got croissants or brioche that need using up, they work too.

AUTUMN

Chocolate cherry roly-poly

This comfort pud favourite gets a Black Forest upgrade with kirsch-soaked cherries and chocolate

Serves 8 • Ready in 1 hr

Butter for greasing
150g (5oz) self-raising flour
50g (2oz) caster sugar
75g (3oz) vegetable suet
Finely grated zest of ½ lemon
75-100ml (3-3½fl oz) milk, plus extra for brushing
100g (3½oz) black cherries in kirsch (we used Opies), drained, roughly chopped and juice reserved
A few whole cherries for decoration
1tbsp cherry or other fruit jam
50g (2oz) chocolate chips
40g (1½oz) flaked almonds
Custard, to serve

1 Heat the oven to 190°C/375°F/Gas 5, and butter a large sheet of baking paper. Mix the flour, sugar, suet and lemon zest in a bowl, then gradually add 75ml (3fl oz) milk, stirring with a knife until it comes together to form a soft dough, adding the remaining milk if the mixture is too dry.
2 Roll out the dough on a floured surface to 30 x 20cm (12 x 8in). Mix the cherries and jam together and spread over the dough, leaving a 2cm (¾in) border. Sprinkle with chocolate chips and almonds. Brush the edges with a little milk, roll up from one short end and pinch the ends to seal.
3 Put the roly-poly on the baking paper, seam-side down, and wrap loosely in the paper, twisting the ends. Place on a baking tray and bake for 25-35 mins until golden. Leave for 5 mins before opening, cut into slices and serve with custard, a drizzle of the reserved cherry juice, and a few whole cherries.
Per serving: Cals 300, Fat 15g, Sat fat 7g, Carbs 36g

Chocolate and amaretto bread and butter pudding

A great Sunday lunch crowd-pleaser dessert

Serves 8 • Ready in 1 hr, plus soaking time

175g (6oz) 70% dark chocolate, broken into squares
80g (3oz) unsalted butter
300ml (10fl oz) single cream
150ml (5fl oz) double cream
100ml (3½fl oz) milk
125g (4½oz) caster sugar
4 eggs, beaten
4tbsp amaretto liqueur
400g (14oz) about 8 slices white bread, crusts removed and each slice cut into 4 triangles
2 amaretti biscuits

1 Put the chocolate, butter, creams, milk and sugar into a pan. Heat very gently, stirring occasionally, until melted and smooth. Remove from the heat and leave to cool for 5 mins.
2 Beat in the eggs and amaretto until combined. Pour a ladleful of the chocolate custard into a 1½l (2½pt) baking dish. Cover with a layer of bread triangles, overlapping them, then add more custard. Repeat the layers, finishing with custard. Press the bread down lightly to make sure it is all covered in custard. Leave to cool, cover and chill for several hours (or overnight if time allows).
3 Heat the oven to 180°C/350°F/Gas 4. Bake, uncovered, for 30 mins. Sprinkle with crushed amaretti biscuits and bake for 5 mins until it is crispy on the outside but soft in the middle. Leave to stand for 5 mins before serving.
Per serving: Cals 609, Fat 37g, Sat fat 21g, Carbs 43g

Plum and hazelnut Bakewell tart

A fabulous twist on a classic

Serves 8 • Ready in 1 hr

375g (13oz) sweet shortcrust pastry, chilled
85g (3oz) butter, softened, plus extra for greasing
85g (3oz) caster sugar
85g (3oz) ground hazelnuts
50g (2oz) self-raising flour
2 eggs, beaten
5tbsp plum jam
12 Victoria plums, halved and pitted
1tbsp caster sugar
You will need:
24cm (9½in) loose-based tart tin

1 Heat the oven to 190°C/375°F/Gas 5 and put a baking tray in the oven to heat. Roll out the pastry on a lightly floured surface to a circle slightly larger than the 24cm (9½in) tart tin. Lift the pastry into the tin and ease it into the base and sides, pressing down lightly. Prick the base with a fork and chill in the fridge.
2 Put the butter, caster sugar, hazelnuts, self-raising flour and eggs in a bowl or food processor and beat or blend until smooth. Spread the jam over the pastry base. Top with the hazelnut mixture and arrange the plums, cut-side up, on top. Sprinkle with caster sugar. Place the tin on the hot baking tray and bake for 30-35 mins until the pastry is cooked and the filling is golden. Leave to cool slightly before serving.
Per serving: Cals 490, Fat 31g, Sat fat 12g, Carbs 45g

TIP This tart lends itself to other delicious flavour combinations too such as pear, blackberry and hazelnut or fig, raspberry and almond.

Plum and hazelnut Bakewell tart

AUTUMN

Caramelised pear and blackberry crumble

TIP Nuts quickly lose their freshness so bring them back to life by toasting them in a hot pan for a few seconds.

Caramelised pear and blackberry crumble

A warming crumble with pecan nuts and cardamom in the topping

Serves 6 • Ready in 50 mins

75g (3oz) butter, cut into small cubes
175g (6oz) self-raising flour
110g (4oz) demerara sugar
100g (3½oz) pecan nuts
1½tsp ground cardamom
6 pears, peeled, quartered and cored
110g (4oz) caster sugar
2tbsp double cream or crème fraîche
200g (7oz) blackberries, fresh or frozen

1 To make the topping, whizz the butter and flour in a food processor to a crumble. Tip into a bowl and add the demerara sugar. Whizz the pecans until finely chopped, add to the crumble mix with ½tsp cardamom and stir well. Chill while you prepare the pears.
2 Melt the caster sugar in pan until you have a pale caramel then add the double cream or crème fraîche and let it bubble for a few minutes.
3 Heat the oven to 170°C/325°F/Gas 5. Put the pears into an ovenproof dish, pour over the caramel, add the blackberries and remaining cardamom, then top with the crumble. Put onto a baking tray and bake for 30-40 mins until golden and bubbling.
Per serving: Cals 585, Fat 26g, Sat fat 9g, Carbs 77g

Rustic plum pie

No need for neatness or a fancy tin here – a simple fruit pie showcasing plums at their best

Serves 6 • Ready in 1 hr, plus chilling

200g (7oz) plain flour, plus extra to dust
125g (4½oz) chilled unsalted butter, cubed
1 medium egg, beaten
100g (3½oz) golden caster sugar
600g (21oz) plums, stoned and cut into chunky slices
Finely grated zest of 1 lemon, plus 1tbsp lemon juice
2tbsp thickening granules
3tbsp plum jam

1 Put the flour and butter into a food processor and whizz until the mixture resembles breadcrumbs. Add the egg, 2tbsp sugar and whizz again until it just forms a ball. Wrap in cling film and chill for 30 mins.
2 Heat the oven to 200°C/400°F/Gas 6. Mix the plums in a bowl with all but 2tsp of the remaining sugar, and the lemon zest and juice.
3 Using a floured rolling pin, roll out the pastry on a large sheet of floured baking paper to a circle about 30cm (12in) across. Lift the pastry and paper onto a baking tray.
4 Sprinkle the centre of the pastry with the thickening granules. Pile the plums in the centre of the pastry, leaving a wide border. Fold the pastry edges up and over the fruit.
5 Sprinkle with the remaining sugar. Bake for 35-40 mins, until the pastry is golden and the fruit is tender. Brush with warm jam to serve.
Per serving: Cals 451, Fat 18g, Sat fat 11g, Carbs 67g

TIP If you don't have thickening granules (we use McDougalls), sprinkle the pastry base with a few breadcrumbs to soak up the juices.

Rustic plum pie

AUTUMN

Halloween TREATS

These new recipes for the spookiest night of the year are scarily good!

Chocolate banoffee sparkler cake

This indulgent showstopper is a perfect end to Halloween

Serves 16 • Ready in 2 hrs, plus cooling time

For the cake:
250g (9oz) unsalted butter, at room temperature
225g (8oz) light muscovado sugar
200g (7oz) golden caster sugar
1tsp vanilla extract
4 large eggs
300g (10½oz) self-raising flour
75g (3oz) cocoa
284ml (9½fl oz) carton buttermilk

For the decoration:
150g (5oz) milk Belgian chocolate
200g (7oz) bar dark chocolate (we used Bournville)
2tsp vegetable oil

For the filling:
2 ripe small bananas
Juice of 1 lemon
250g (9oz) mascarpone
50g (2oz) icing sugar, sieved
2tbsp vanilla extract
397g (14oz) can caramel

You will need:
3 x 19cm (7½in) sandwich tins, greased and base lined
Indoor sparklers

1 Heat the oven to 160°C/320°F/Gas 3. Put the butter, sugars and vanilla into the bowl of an electric mixer. Beat for 10 mins. Gradually add the eggs, beating well between each addition.
2 Add ½ the flour, cocoa and buttermilk and combine. Repeat, adding the remaining ingredients.
3 Spoon the mixture into the tins and bake for 45 mins.
4 Melt the milk and dark chocolates in 2 bowls, resting over pans of simmering water each with 1tsp oil.
5 Tip dark chocolate into a margarine tub, then drizzle in the milk chocolate and swirl together with a skewer. Chill for at least 1 hr.
6 To make the curls, tip the block of chocolate on to a baking paper-lined tray. Drag a cheese slicer over the chocolate to create huge curls. Put on to the tray and chill.
7 Slice the bananas and squeeze on the lemon juice. Meanwhile, stir the mascarpone, icing sugar and vanilla extract together until smooth.
8 Cool the cakes on a wire rack, peeling away the lining paper. Just before serving, put the cake on to a serving plate, spread over ½ the mascarpone filling, top with ½ the well-drained bananas and ½ the caramel. Repeat with another cake layer and sandwich with the final cake. Use a palette knife to arrange the curls on top. Push the indoor sparklers in the cake and light to serve.
Per serving: Cals 607, Fat 31g, Sat fat 19g, Carbs 73g

Chocolate banoffee sparkler cake

HALLOWEEN TREATS

Toffee apples with a twist

We've given this recipe a Halloween makeover by coating the skins in vampire-black syrup

Makes 10 • Ready in 30 mins

10 Granny Smith apples
800g (1lb 12oz) golden caster sugar
½ a tube of extra-strong black food colouring (we used Dr Oetker)
2tsp vinegar
8tbsp golden syrup

1 Place the apples in a bowl of boiling water to remove the waxy coating. Dry thoroughly and remove the stalks. Push a wooden lolly stick or clean twig through the stalk hole, halfway into the core of the apple.
2 Put 100ml (3½fl oz) water in a small pan with the sugar and the food colouring over a medium heat. Allow the sugar to dissolve, then add the vinegar and golden syrup. Insert a sugar thermometer into the pan and heat until it reaches 150°C/300°F/Gas 2. While the sugar is still hot, tilt the pan and dip and twist the apples in the toffee mixture, one at a time. Place on a greased baking tray with space between them, and leave to cool before serving with twigs or kebab sticks to hold.
Per serving: Cals 654, Fat 9g, Sat fat 1.5g, Carbs 95g

Cobweb chocolate tart

Thanks to our friend the food processor, this tart is amazingly simple and quick to make. It's a great one to whizz up for a Halloween-themed supper, and always sure to impress

Serves 8 • Ready in 45 mins

300g (10½oz) dark chocolate
300ml (10fl oz) double cream
1 all-butter pastry case
3 marshmallows

1 Break the chocolate into small pieces and place in a food processor. Heat the double cream until it's steaming, pour it over the chocolate and blitz until the mixture is smooth and all the chocolate has melted.
2 Pour the chocolate mixture into the pastry case. Place in the fridge to set for 30 mins.
3 Put the marshmallows in a microwave-proof bowl and microwave for 30 secs. Leave to cool slightly, then use your thumb and forefinger to pull strings across the top of the chocolate tart, creating a spiderweb effect.
Per serving: Cals 520, Fat 38g, Sat fat 21g, Carbs 38g

TIP You need to assemble this cake at the last minute to guarantee it stays looking its best!

SEASONAL COOKBOOK woman&home 115

Fireworks FEAST

These tasty autumn warmers are perfect for a Bonfire Night gathering

TIP Don't slice the apples for the top too far in advance as they will start to discolour.

Toffee apple tart

FIREWORKS FEAST

Toffee apple tart

Turn everyone's favourite Bonfire Night treat into this elegant dessert!

Serves 8 • Ready in 2 hrs, plus chilling

375g (13oz) sweet shortcrust pastry
1kg (2lb) Bramley apples, peeled, cored and chopped into small chunks
100g (3½oz) butter
A pinch of cinnamon
125g (4½oz) caster sugar plus 2tbsp extra
Zest of ½ a lemon
2tbsp cornflour
3 dessert apples, peeled, cored, quartered and finely sliced

For the caramel sauce:
65g (2½oz) caster sugar
15g (1tbsp) salted butter
2tbsp double cream
Crème fraîche, to serve

1 Heat the oven to 180°C/350°F/Gas 4. Roll the pastry out to around 3mm (⅛in) thick, and line a 23cm (9in) tart tin with it, pinching the edge to crimp. Prick the pastry base and chill for 30 mins.
2 Put the apples, 4tbsp water and the butter in a pan over a low heat until the butter melts. Add the cinnamon.
3 Increase the heat and cook for 30 mins. Blitz in a food processor until smooth. Whisk in the sugar, lemon zest and cornflour, and cook on a low heat, stirring, until thickened. Remove from the heat and set aside.
4 Line the chilled pastry with baking paper. Fill with baking beans and bake for 20 mins. Remove beans and baking paper and bake for 10 mins.
5 Evenly spread the apple filling over the baked pastry case. Arrange the dessert apples, overlapping slightly, on top in a spiral, working inwards. Bake for 30 mins more.
6 Meanwhile, put the sugar in a large pan over a medium heat and cook until it's a caramel colour. Remove from the heat and whisk in the butter. Once smooth, add the cream.
7 Brush the caramel sauce over the pie and leave to set. Serve with dollops of crème fraîche.
Per serving: Cals 549, Fat 29g, Sat fat 14g, Carbs 65g

Pulled pork baps

Let the oven do the hard work

Serves 8 • Ready in 3 hrs 30 mins

3 onions, chopped
3 garlic cloves, crushed
A few sprigs of thyme (optional)
2tsp sea salt
2tsp Creole or Cajun seasoning
1kg (2lb) boneless pork shoulder, skin scored
3tbsp balsamic vinegar
600ml (20fl oz) chicken stock
8 white baps
4 tomatoes, sliced
Watercress (optional)
½ bottle barbecue sauce, such as Levi Roots Reggae Reggae Mild Sauce, to serve

1 Heat the oven to 240°C/475°F/Gas 9. Put the onions, garlic and thyme in a roasting tin. Rub the salt and seasoning over the pork and place on the onions.
2 Cook for 30 mins. Turn the oven down to 140°C/275°F/Gas 1. Pour the vinegar and stock into the tin, cover with foil and cook for 2 hrs 45 mins.
3 Use two forks to shred the pork. Serve in baps with the tomatoes, watercress, if using, and the sauce.
Per serving: Cals 454, Fat 10g, Sat fat 3g, Carbs 52g

DAIRY FREE

Pulled pork baps

Quorn chilli pitta pockets

These spiced vegetarian pittas are great for a cool evening

Serves 6 • Ready in 30 mins

2tbsp sunflower oil
1 red onion, chopped
1tbsp chipotle paste
1 garlic clove, crushed
500g (17½oz) frozen Quorn mince
400g (14oz) can chopped tomatoes
300ml (10fl oz) vegetable stock
420g (15oz) can Mexican mixed beans
6 pitta breads
1 avocado, mashed
100ml (3½fl oz) soured cream

1 Heat the sunflower oil in a pan and fry the red onion for a few mins. Add the chipotle paste, crushed garlic and Quorn mince, and cook for 5 mins.
2 Stir in the tomatoes, vegetable stock and Mexican mixed beans. Season and simmer for 15 mins.
3 To serve, toast and split the pittas. Spoon in the chilli and top with avocado and soured cream.
Per serving: Cals 479, Fat 15g, Sat fat 4.5g, Carbs 59g

Quorn chilli pitta pockets

WINTER

118 woman&home SEASONAL COOKBOOK

WINTER

Winter

- 122 Sparkling wine and pomegranate jelly
- 122 Celery and pomegranate salad
- 123 Rose petal chicken with pomegranate
- 123 Winter pavlova
- 126 Cauliflower soup with bacon and croutons
- 127 Red chicory, walnut and goat's cheese salad
- 129 Perfect roast turkey
- 129 Gravy
- 129 Bread sauce
- 130 Stir-fried Brussels sprouts with lemon and garlic
- 130 Sweet sesame roast carrots
- 130 Roast potatoes and parsnips
- 130 Braised red cabbage
- 130 Chestnut, apple and red onion stuffing
- 133 Asian sticky salmon
- 133 Two-cheese and onion tart
- 133 Gingerbread spiced ham
- 136 Roast beef with a mustard and thyme crust
- 137 Vegetable and truffle tartlets
- 142 Chocolate and amaretto yule log
- 142 Tropical "mess"
- 143 Vegan figgy puds
- 146 Chocolate orange trifle
- 146 Christmas bombe
- 147 Raspberry meringue bombe
- 149 Miso prawn skewers
- 151 Asian sausage rolls
- 151 Smoked salmon filo bites
- 152 Fondue with mini roasties
- 152 Spiced lamb koftas with minty cucumber raita
- 154 Tikka prawn poppadom bites
- 155 A trio of dips
- 157 Mexican meatballs
- 157 Cheese straws
- 158 Jammy heart dodgers
- 159 Berry tart
- 160 Multigrain pancakes with poached rhubarb
- 160 Ice-cream sundae crepe
- 161 Tiramisu crepe cake

WINTER

Winter in SEASON

Winter is a great time to find colourful produce to brighten up your festive feasts

✢ APPLES
Perfect in crumbles and tarts, they also make a great addition to stuffing and festive cheeseboards.

✢ BRUSSELS SPROUTS
As long as they're not overcooked, they're a must – lightly steam, then stir-fry with pancetta and chestnuts.

✢ CABBAGE
The red variety looks particularly festive – try it cooked with traditional spices, or shredded into a healthy coleslaw.

✢ CELERIAC
Such an underused root veg, it has a very subtle celery flavour and is great baked with parsnips, or made into a creamy mash to serve with a hearty beef casserole.

✢ CHESTNUTS
Slightly sweeter and lower in fat than other nuts, add chopped, toasted chestnuts to cookie dough along with cinnamon and nutmeg.

✢ CLEMENTINES, SATSUMAS AND TANGERINES
At their best during the winter months, these citrus fruits make for a welcome healthy snack in-between all that rich party food.

✢ CRANBERRIES
The classic accompaniment to turkey, these colourful, antioxidant-rich berries can also be added to chutney or made into a compote and stirred through Greek yoghurt. They freeze well too – try making ice cubes with them to add to cocktails.

✢ DUCK AND GOOSE
These make the perfect roast. Buy the best quality you can afford as pasture-reared birds have higher levels of Omega-3 fatty acids. We love Goodman's Geese and Riverford.

✢ HORSERADISH
Serving a selection of cold meats and breads on Boxing Day? Pep up that sandwich with horseradish sauce: simply stir crème fraîche, lemon juice and a pinch of sugar through grated horseradish and season to taste.

✢ NUTS IN THE SHELL
Brazils, walnuts, almonds, hazelnuts, pecans… Keep the nutcracker handy for an easy protein boost. Shelling them yourself means you're less likely to eat as many.

✢ PARSNIPS
At their best roasted, choose smaller ones for a sweeter taste. Toss them with a little honey and goose fat for a flavoursome, crispy glaze.

✢ PEARS
Mix with walnuts, Stilton and salad leaves, and drizzle with balsamic vinegar for an easy-to-assemble starter, or serve with a cheeseboard.

✢ PUMPKIN AND SQUASH
Roast first for a more intense flavour, then purée into soup or dice and add to risotto. Don't throw pumpkin seeds away – spread on an oiled baking tray and roast with a little salt.

Coming soon…
Blood oranges come into season just after Christmas. Delicious for juicing or for making our fab cheesecake on womanandhome.com

POMEGRANATE
Scatter this jewel-like fruit over cheesecake for a festive finish, or make a wintry cocktail by mixing the juice with gin and topping up with Prosecco

WINTER

Sparkling wine and pomegranate jelly

Impress guests with a lovely grown-up jelly recipe

Serves 6 • Ready in 25 mins, plus setting

1 pomegranate
100ml (3½fl oz) pomegranate juice
7 gelatine leaves
500ml (17fl oz) sparkling wine
Edible rose petals, to decorate
You will need
6 glasses

1 Halve the pomegranate then hold each half over a bowl and bash the skins with a rolling pin to loosen the seeds. Scoop out the seeds into the bowl and remove any pith. Divide between the glasses.
2 Warm the pomegranate juice in a small pan. Meanwhile soak the gelatine leaves in cold water for 5mins to soften. Take the pan off the heat, shake the excess water from the gelatine and stir it into the pomegranate juice until dissolved. Stir in the sparkling wine and pour into the glasses. Chill in the fridge for at least 4 hrs until set. Decorate with edible rose petals and serve.
Per serving: Cals 94, Fat 0g, Carbs 9g

Celery and pomegranate salad

Celery and pomegranate salad

To make a more substantial salad, add some crumbled feta cheese or griddled halloumi cheese

Serves 6 • Ready in 10 mins

75g (3oz) pack of watercress, washed
4 celery sticks, peeled and sliced
250g (9oz) pack cooked beetroot (not in vinegar), sliced
A small handful of mint leaves
50g (2oz) ready-prepared pomegranate seeds or seeds from 1 pomegranate
For the dressing
6tbsp pomegranate juice
Juice of ½ lemon
1tsp Dijon mustard
6tbsp olive oil

1 Place the watercress, celery, beetroot, mint and pomegranate seeds in a large serving bowl.
2 Place all the dressing ingredients in a screw-top jar and season with salt and freshly ground black pepper. Shake well to mix and pour over the salad just before serving.
Per serving: Cals 134, Fat 11g, Sat fat 2g, Carbs 7g

Sparkling wine and pomegranate jelly

WINTER IN SEASON

Rose petal chicken with pomegranate

Winter pavlova

As fruits have different nutrient profiles, eating a wide variety, and choosing from those that are in season, gives optimum benefits

Serves 8 • Ready in 1 hr 45 mins, plus cooling

5 large egg whites
300g (10½oz) caster sugar
½tsp vinegar
1tbsp cornflour, sifted
500ml (17fl oz) Greek yoghurt
1tsp vanilla extract
500g (1lb) fruit in season, such as peaches and plums, halved, stoned and sliced; blackberries; and pomegranate seeds
You will need
A baking tray lined with baking paper

1 Heat the oven to 140°C/275°F/Gas 1. In a large clean bowl, whisk the egg whites until stiff peaks form. Gradually beat in the sugar, a little at a time, until the mixture is thick and glossy, then fold in the vinegar and cornflour.
2 Secure the baking paper on the baking tray with a drop of the mixture in each corner. Spoon on the remaining mixture to form a circle about 23cm (9in) in diameter. Cook for 1 hr 30 mins, or until the outside is crisp. Turn off the oven, but leave the meringue inside for 1 hr, then remove to cool completely.
3 When cold and ready to serve, stir the yoghurt and vanilla extract together, spoon over the meringue and top with the fruit.
Per serving: Cals 260, Fat 6.5g, Sat fat 4g, Carbs 44g

Rose petal chicken with pomegranate

This is deliciously spicy but it won't blow your head off!

Serves 4 • Ready in 1 hr, plus overnight marinating

1kg (2lb) free-range chicken thighs, skin on, bone in
4tbsp olive oil, plus a little extra
3tbsp dried rose petals (find them in Waitrose), blended to a powder
1tbsp ground cumin
2tbsp ground coriander
1tbsp fennel seeds, crushed
1tsp chilli flakes
For the salad
250g (9oz) bulgar wheat, cooked
4 preserved lemons, finely chopped
110g (4oz) pomegranate seeds
4tbsp chopped fresh coriander
Juice of 1 lemon
3tbsp olive oil

1 Put the chicken thighs in a large bowl. Add the remaining ingredients, mix well, cover and leave to marinate overnight.
2 Heat the oven to 200°C/400°F/Gas 6. Put the chicken pieces and marinade in a shallow roasting tin, and drizzle over a little oil and some sea salt. Bake for 1 hr.
3 Mix together all the salad ingredients with plenty of seasoning and serve with the chicken.
Per serving: Cals 748, Fat 36g, Sat fat 6g, Carbs 51g

Winter pavlova

SEASONAL COOKBOOK **woman&home** 123

WINTER

A CHRISTMAS FEAST

A CHRISTMAS FEAST

There's no need to panic this December – stay on track for the best festive lunch with our simple countdown

For traditionalists, our Perfect roast turkey with all the trimmings will be a triumph

Fancy an alternative? Try Gingerbread spiced ham, Asian sticky salmon or our fabulous veggie options

Cauliflower soup with bacon and croutons

Cauliflower soup with bacon and croutons

This velvety smooth soup is naturally rich and creamy, so keep servings small

Easy/prepare ahead
- Serves 8 • Ready in 30 mins

70g (2½oz) butter
1 onion, chopped
2 sticks of celery, chopped
2 cauliflower, broken into florets
2 bay leaves
670ml (22½fl oz) hot vegetable stock
670ml (22½fl oz) whole milk
A grating of nutmeg
135ml (4½fl oz) single cream

To serve
Crispy bacon, croutons, crème fraîche and chives

1 Melt the butter in a saucepan, then add the onion and celery and cook gently until soft. Add the cauliflower florets, bay leaves, stock, milk and nutmeg, and season generously with salt and freshly ground black pepper. Bring to the boil, then simmer for 20 mins.
2 Add the cream, then whizz in a blender until smooth. Serve with crispy bacon, croutons, crème fraîche, chives and a grinding of black pepper.

Per serving: Cals 225, Fat 14g, Sat Fat 9g, Carbs 13g

A CHRISTMAS FEAST

Red chicory, walnut and goat's cheese salad

This warm, wintry salad is perfect for a light Christmas Day starter

Easy/prepare ahead
Serves 4 • Ready in 20 mins

2tbsp olive oil
2 handfuls of walnuts
3 heads of red chicory, leaves separated
400g (14oz) unrinded goat's cheese, broken into chunks
6 sprigs of thyme, leaves removed
3tbsp white wine vinegar
6tbsp walnut oil
A pinch of sugar

1 Heat the olive oil in a frying pan, then add the walnuts with some sea salt and cook, tossing, for 3-4 mins until toasted and crisp. Allow to cool slightly, then divide the chicory, goat's cheese and thyme leaves between 4 plates, and scatter the walnuts over.
2 Mix the vinegar, walnut oil and sugar, season and drizzle over the salads.
Per serving: Cals 612, Fat 57g, Sat fat 22g, Carbs 3g

> **TIP**
> To turn this into a main course over the festive season, serve with chicken or duck breast – crisp the skin in a hot pan, then finish off in the oven.

Perfect roast turkey

HOW TO CARVE
It may not look quite as impressive, but it's easier to joint the turkey than to carve it whole at the table. Take off the legs and slice into thighs and drumsticks. Then ease off the breast with a sharp knife, starting at the breastbone and working down; slice them too. Visit womanandhome.com for a how-to video.

A CHRISTMAS FEAST

Perfect roast turkey

Invest in a digital meat thermometer so you leave nothing to chance and everything to science! In general terms, allow 20 mins per kg, adding 70 mins more cooking time if it's under under 4kg, and 90 mins if it's over 4kg

Easy • Serves 6-8 • Ready in 2 hrs 40 mins

1 bunch of fresh thyme
1 onion, peeled and quartered
1 lemon, quartered
2 fresh bay leaves
4kg (8lb) free-range turkey
75g (3oz) butter
For the gravy
600ml (20fl oz) rich turkey or chicken stock
300ml (10fl oz) Amontillado sherry or white wine
2tsp cornflour

1 Heat the oven to 200°C/400°F/Gas 6. Stuff the thyme, onion, lemon and bay leaves into the turkey cavity. Rub the butter all over the skin and season well. Put in a roasting tin and roast for 20 mins.
2 Turn down the oven temperature to 180°C/350°F/Gas 4. Cover the turkey loosely with foil and roast for around 2 hrs. Use a meat thermometer to check the temperature; it should be a minimum of 75°C/167°F. Alternatively, the juices should run clear when you pierce the thickest part of the thigh. Put on a dish, cover with foil and rest for 30 mins to 1 hr before carving. Strain off the pan juices.
Per serving: Cals 351-325, Fat 10-9g, Sat fat 4-3g saturated, Carbs 4-3g

Gravy (serves 8)
Bring the stock and sherry to the boil in a large pan and add the turkey juices. Bubble for 10 mins. Mix the cornflour with a little cold water and add to the pan, stirring to thicken.

Bread sauce (serves 8)
Put **300ml (10fl oz) chicken** or **turkey stock** and **300ml (10fl oz) milk** into a pan and heat. Add **1 onion**, peeled, halved and studded with **10-15 cloves**, **1 bay leaf** and **10 black peppercorns**. Bring to the boil, remove from the heat and leave to infuse for 2 hrs. Strain, add **125g (4½oz) fresh white breadcrumbs** and cook gently for 10 mins, stirring occasionally, until thickened. Season. To serve, add **35g (1¼oz) unsalted butter**, **2tbsp double cream** and a grating of **nutmeg**; reheat gently.

TIP When it comes to the turkey, the best advice is to buy the best bird you can afford

WINTER

Stir-fried Brussels sprouts with lemon and garlic
Easy • Serves 8 • Ready in 25 mins

- 2tbsp olive oil • 3 garlic cloves, finely chopped • 750g (1lb 10oz) Brussels sprouts, trimmed and roughly chopped • Zest of 1 lemon

Heat the oil in a large non-stick pan or wok and fry the garlic for 2 mins. Add the sprouts. Don't move them around the pan for 1 min to allow the edges to brown, then toss. Carry on stir-frying until golden. Sprinkle the lemon zest onto the sprouts before serving.
Per serving: Cals 75, Fat 4g, Sat fat 0.7g, Carbs 4g

Sweet sesame roast carrots
Easy/Prepare ahead • Serves 8 • Ready in 1 hr

- 500g (17½oz) carrots, peeled and cut into batons • ½tbsp olive oil • 1tbsp runny honey • 2tbsp sesame seeds • 1½tsp ground ginger

Mix the carrots with the olive oil, honey, sesame seeds and ground ginger. Put on a baking tray and roast in a 200°C/400°F/Gas 6 oven for 50 mins until golden.
Per serving: Cals 66, Fat 4g, Sat fat 1g, Carbs 5g

Roast potatoes and parsnips
Easy/prepare ahead
- Serves 8 • Ready in 1 hr 20 mins

- 1½kg (3lb) potatoes, peeled and quartered • 8tbsp rapeseed oil • 800g (1lb 12oz) parsnips, peeled and halved • 2tsp chopped thyme

1 Put the potatoes in a pan with cold water. Bring to the boil, simmer for 6 mins, drain and steam-dry for 3 mins. Shake the potatoes to fluff the edges and toss with 6tbsp of the oil.
2 Mix the parsnips with the remaining oil. Roast the potatoes in a roasting tin, in a 200°C/400°F/Gas 6 oven for 15 mins, then add the parsnips. Return to the oven to cook for 30 mins, turning occasionally.
3 Sprinkle the thyme over the potatoes and parsnips, pop back into the oven and roast for a further 15 mins.
Per serving: Cals 482, Fat 21g, Sat fat 5g, Carbs 55g

Braised red cabbage
Freeze • Serves 8 • Ready in 2 hrs 15 mins

- 1kg (2lb) red cabbage, shredded • 350g (12oz) Bramley apples, peeled, cored and roughly chopped • 2 red onions, sliced • 3tbsp soft brown sugar • 3tbsp balsamic vinegar • 1tsp each ground nutmeg, cloves and cinnamon • 1 cinnamon stick (optional) • 50g (2oz) butter, cut into small cubes

Layer up all the ingredients, except the butter, seasoning as you go, in a large pan. Dot the butter over the surface. Cover and cook on the hob on a low heat for 2 hrs, stirring occasionally.
Per serving: Cals 147, Fat 6g, Sat fat 3g, Carbs 19g

Chestnut, apple and red onion stuffing
Easy/prepare ahead
- Serves 8 • Ready in 1 hr

- 60g (2½oz) butter • 3 red onions, finely chopped • 2 garlic cloves, crushed • 2 Braeburn apples, cored and chopped • 200ml (7fl oz) sherry • 1tbsp fresh sage or thyme, chopped • 200g (7oz) fresh breadcrumbs • 200g (7oz) chestnuts, chopped

1 Melt the butter in a pan, then cook the onions gently for 15 mins until golden.
2 Add the garlic and the apples. Cook for 2 mins, then stir in the sherry. Bubble for 3 mins.
3 Stir the sage, breadcrumbs and chestnuts into the apple mix, season, then press into a buttered dish. Bake in a 200°C/400°F/Gas 6 oven for 20 mins until golden.
Per serving: Cals 259, Fat 7.5g, Sat fat 4g, Carbs 36g

A CHRISTMAS FEAST

TIP
Add a teaspoon or two of orange zest to cranberry sauce – perfect with the turkey.

TIP
Wow a crowd over Christmas with this spicy new take on roasted salmon – a wonderful buffet centrepiece dish.

Asian sticky salmon

A CHRISTMAS FEAST

Asian sticky salmon

This simple yet impressive salmon recipe is great for feeding a crowd

Easy/Prepare ahead
• Serves 8-10 • Ready in 35 mins, plus marinating

1 whole side of salmon
Coriander, finely chopped, red chilli, deseeded and finely chopped, and lime wedges, to serve
For the marinade
2tbsp soy sauce
2tbsp honey
2tbsp rice wine vinegar
4tbsp hoisin sauce
2 star anise
2tsp each Thai 7 spice and Thai fish sauce
2 garlic cloves, crushed

1 Mix all the marinade ingredients together. Put the salmon on a large piece of foil, bring the edges up to form a boat around it, pour over the marinade and scrunch the edges of the foil together. Leave in the fridge to marinate for at least 6 hrs, or overnight.
2 To cook, heat the oven to 220°C/425°F/Gas 7. Remove the salmon from the marinade and put on a well oiled double piece of foil in a roasting tin. Roast in the oven for 15-20 mins, depending on whether you want it opaque in the middle or completely cooked.
3 Meanwhile, transfer the marinade to a pan, bring to the boil and simmer for a few mins until thick and syrupy. Pour over the salmon for the last 5 mins of cooking, then, when sticky and slightly caramelised, transfer the fish to a serving platter and scatter with the chopped coriander and chilli. Serve with lime wedges.
Per serving: Cals 219-175, Fat 12-10g, Sat fat 2-1.7g, Carbs 4-3g

Two-cheese and onion tart

Using different types of cheese gives plenty of depth to this quiche, with red onion marmalade delivering a sweet note

Easy/Prepare ahead
• Serves 6 • Ready in 1 hr 10 mins

375g (13oz) ready-rolled all-butter shortcrust pastry
130ml (4fl oz) double cream
130ml (4fl oz) milk
50g (2oz) Cheddar
1 egg, plus 2 egg yolks
200g (7oz) Stilton, broken into chunks
3-5tbsp red onion marmalade
You will need
A 20cm (8in) fluted loose-based flan tin, lightly oiled, and baking beans

1 Heat the oven to 200°C/400°F/Gas 6. Use the pastry to line the flan tin. Chill, then bake blind for around 20 mins until it's cooked through. Allow to cool slightly.
2 Meanwhile, mix the cream, milk, most of the Cheddar, egg and egg yolks, and season well. Turn the oven down to 150°C/300°F/Gas 2. Scatter the Stilton over the pastry case. Spoon over the red onion marmalade, then pour the egg mixture into the pastry case until it almost reaches the top. Scatter the remaining Cheddar on top, then bake for 40-45 mins until the quiche is just set. Allow to cool slightly and either serve warm or at room temperature. It will keep in the fridge for up to 3 days.
Per serving: Cals 620, Fat 47g, Sat fat 24g, Carbs 33g

> TIP It doesn't have to be all about meat. This rich, flavoursome tart is perfect for vegetarians

Gingerbread spiced ham

Wonderfully Christmassy, this is ideal for a buffet as it's delicious hot or cold

Easy/Prepare ahead • Serves 10-12 •
Ready in 2 hrs 30 mins

4kg (9lb) uncooked ham (smoked or unsmoked), off the bone
1 onion, roughly chopped
1 carrot, roughly chopped
1 stick of celery, roughly chopped
6 black peppercorns
1 bay leaf
Cloves, to stud
For the glaze
4tbsp marmalade
¼tsp allspice
1tsp ginger
½tsp mixed spice

1 Rinse the ham well, then put in a deep saucepan and cover with cold water. Bring to the boil, then drain (this removes the scum), rinse again and return to the clean pan, along with the onion, carrot, celery, peppercorns and bay leaf. Cover with cold water once more, bring to the boil, then simmer very gently for 1 hr 40 mins.
2 Heat the oven to 200°C/400°F/Gas 6. Take the ham out of the cooking liquid, then remove the top layer of skin, leaving the soft fat in place (keep the skin for crackling). Score diamonds into the fat and stud with cloves at the point of each diamond. Mix together the glaze ingredients and brush thickly over the ham. Bake for 30 mins until golden brown and bubbling. Allow to cool slightly, then serve either warm or at room temperature.
3 To make the crackling, put the skin over an upturned cake tin on top of a baking tray. This allows the trapped hot air inside the tin to cook the skin from underneath so it crisps more easily. Sprinkle well with salt, then cook in an oven turned to its highest setting for 20-25 mins until golden and bubbling. Break the crackling into pieces and serve with warm apple sauce as an appetising pre-dinner nibble.
Per serving: Cals 831-693, Fat 49-41g, Sat fat 16-14g saturated, Carbs 4-3.5g

SEASONAL COOKBOOK woman&home 133

WINTER

Two-cheese and onion tart

134 woman&home SEASONAL COOKBOOK

A CHRISTMAS FEAST

Gingerbread spiced ham

WINTER

Roast beef with a mustard and thyme crust

Resting the meat ensures even cooking, and you don't lose the juices as you carve

Easy/Prepare ahead • Serves 6-8 • Ready in 1 hr 30 mins

1½kg (3lb) topside of beef, the fat lightly scored
4tbsp gluten-free grainy mustard
½tbsp light soft brown sugar
2tbsp port
4 sprigs of thyme, leaves only

1 Heat the oven to 200°C/400°F/Gas 6. Put the beef into a roasting tin (on a roasting rack, if you have one). In a bowl, mix together the mustard and sugar, and season well with salt and freshly ground black pepper. Spread the mixture all over the top of the beef, covering the outside layer of fat.
2 Pour the port into the roasting tin. Transfer to the oven for 20 mins, then reduce the temperature to 170°C/325°F/Gas 3, and cook for 1 hr for medium rare, or 1 hr 15 mins for well done. Sprinkle the beef with the thyme for the final 15 mins of cooking time. Leave to rest for at least 15 mins before carving.
Per serving: Cals 319-236, Fat 8-6g, Sat fat 3-2g, Carbs 2-1.5g

A CHRISTMAS FEAST

Vegetable and truffle tartlets

These go beautifully with all the Christmas trimmings

Easy/Prepare ahead
• Makes 6 • Ready in 1 hr 30 mins, plus chilling

450g (1lb) shortcrust pastry
100g (3½oz) Jerusalem artichokes
Juice of 1 lemon
100g (3½oz) sweet potato, peeled and cut into chunks
25g (1oz) unsalted butter
25g (1oz) plain flour
200ml (7fl oz) whole milk
50g (2oz) mature Cheddar cheese, finely grated
½tsp truffle oil
2 thyme sprigs, leaves only, finely chopped
3 large eggs, separated

For the breadcrumb topping
25g (1oz) butter
60g (2½oz) breadcrumbs
2 garlic cloves, crushed
A handful of parsley leaves, finely chopped, and red amaranth or micro herbs (from Marks & Spencer), to garnish

You will need
6 x 10cm (2½ x 4in) tart tins and baking beans

1 Line the tart tins with the pastry, leaving the overlapping edge untrimmed. Chill for at least 30 mins in the fridge. Heat the oven to 200°C/400°F/Gas 6. Peel the Jerusalem artichokes and put immediately into a pan of water with the lemon juice. Cook the sweet potato with the artichokes for 20 mins or until tender. Drain, then set aside to cool slightly. Blend to a purée.
2 Trim the excess pastry to create a neat edge. Line with foil and fill with baking beans. Bake for 20 mins; set aside to cool. Melt the butter in a small saucepan over a medium heat. Add the flour, cook for 1 min, then gradually add the milk, stirring continuously, until smooth. Stir in the cheese, truffle oil and thyme leaves, along with plenty of seasoning. Remove from the heat, stir in the puréed vegetables and egg yolks. Set aside to cool slightly.
3 Reduce the oven to 180°C/350°F/Gas 4. Whisk the egg whites until stiff, fold into the egg yolk mixture and divide between the tartlets. Bake for 20 mins.
4 For the breadcrumbs, put the butter in a frying pan over a medium heat. Let it foam for 30 secs, then add the garlic and breadcrumbs. Fry until golden, then season. Take off the heat and stir in the parsley. Sprinkle over the tarts to serve, and garnish with red amaranth, if using.
Per serving: Cals 591, Fat 38g, Sat fat 17g, Carbs 45g

TIP
Make the tartlets the day before and store, covered, in the fridge. Fry off the crumbs but don't add them until you reheat the tarts for 15 mins at 200°C/400°F/Gas 6.

Vegetable and truffle tartlets

WINTER

SOMETHING SWEET

Winter is the season to tempt guests with something extra special – take your pick from our mouthwatering selection

From stunning centrepieces to Christmas pudding with a difference and a new way to serve panettone

These desserts are super indulgent so keep portion sizes small… you can always come back for more!

SEASONAL COOKBOOK **woman&home** 139

WINTER

Chocolate and amaretto yule log

SOMETHING SWEET

Tropical "mess"

SEASONAL COOKBOOK woman&home 141

WINTER

Chocolate and amaretto yule log

The amaretto can be left out of the recipe if you're feeding under-18s

Prepare ahead
- Serves 10-12 • Ready in 1 hr

6 large eggs, separated
125g (4½oz) caster sugar
50g (2oz) cocoa powder, plus 1tbsp extra
For the chocolate mousse filling
200g (7oz) plain chocolate, broken into chunks
25g (1oz) unsalted butter, at room temperature
4 large eggs, separated
2tbsp amaretto
75g (3oz) caster sugar
200ml (7fl oz) half-fat double cream
For the almond brittle
50g (2oz) caster sugar
35g (1¼oz) blanched almonds, toasted and roughly chopped
Icing sugar, to decorate
You will need
A 30x20cm (12x8in) deep-sided rectangular tin, lined with baking paper

1 To make the sponge, heat the oven to 170°C/325°F/Gas 3. Put the egg yolks and sugar in a bowl, and whisk with an electric mixer until pale and thick. Sift the cocoa powder over the top and fold in.
2 In a separate bowl, whisk the egg whites until very stiff. Fold into the yolks; add a tbsp first to loosen the mixture, then gradually add the rest until well combined. Pour into the tin, and bake on the centre shelf of the oven for 15-20 mins, until well risen and springy to the touch.
3 Remove the sponge from the oven, sprinkle with the remaining cocoa, put a sheet of baking paper on top and invert onto a chopping board. Peel off the lining paper, and roll up the roulade tightly from the long side, using the baking paper to help you. Set aside.
4 For the mousse filling, put the chocolate in a heatproof bowl set over a pan of simmering water. When melted, remove from the heat and stir in the butter. Leave to cool slightly. Stir in the egg yolks and amaretto and mix well. In a clean bowl, whisk the egg whites until stiff, then gradually whisk in the sugar until the mixture is thick and glossy. Fold the egg whites into the chocolate mixture. In a clean bowl, whip the cream until soft peaks form.
5 To make the almond brittle, oil a baking tray and keep to hand. Put the sugar in a saucepan and gently heat without stirring until the sugar dissolves. Increase the heat and boil for 2-3 mins or until it turns a light golden brown. Stir occasionally to make sure it doesn't crystallise. Tilt the pan now and then to ensure it all melts. Spread out the almonds on the baking tray. Pour over the caramel, allow to cool completely then break into shards.
6 To assemble, unroll the roulade and spread with a good layer of the mousse filling, reserving the rest for the top. Spread the whipped cream gently over the mousse, and then re-roll the roulade as tightly as possible, using the paper to help you. Spread the remaining mousse all over the roulade and fork all over to produce a log effect. Use the shards of almond brittle to decorate the top of the roulade. Dust with icing sugar and serve.
Per serving: Cals 530-442, Fat 27-22.5g, Sat fat 14-11g, Carbs 67-55g

TIP The roulade will keep in the fridge for up to 2 days – just add the almond brittle when serving

Tropical "mess"

Our Christmas version of Eton mess, which is much tangier and makes the most of tropical fruits

Easy/Prepare ahead
- Serves 8
- Ready in 1 hr, plus cooling

3 large egg whites
175g (6oz) light soft brown sugar
2tbsp toasted chopped hazelnuts
A selection of tropical fruit, chopped (such as mango, passion fruit, pineapple, papaya, kiwi fruit, pomegranate seeds, physalis)
300ml (10fl oz) double cream, lightly whipped
Pomegranate molasses, to serve
You will need
2 baking trays, lined with baking paper

1 Heat the oven to 150°C/300°F/Gas 2. Put the egg whites in the bowl of an electric mixer and whisk on a slow speed until frothy. Increase the speed and whisk until very stiff, then start adding the sugar, a dessert spoonful at a time, until the mixture is very thick and glossy.
2 Fold in 1tbsp of the hazelnuts. Spoon 12 heaped dessert spoonfuls of meringue onto the baking trays, allowing a little room for them to expand. Sprinkle the remaining hazelnuts on top and bake for 40 mins. Turn off the oven and allow to cool completely. Store in an airtight tin for up to 5 days.
3 Mix three-quarters of the fruit with the whipped cream and lightly crushed meringue, then spoon into glass dishes and top with the remaining fruit. Drizzle with pomegranate molasses to serve.
Per serving: Cals 356, Fat 23g, Sat fat 13g, Carbs 33g

142 woman&home SEASONAL COOKBOOK

SOMETHING SWEET

Vegan figgy puds

These are delicious served with a scoop of non-dairy ice cream

Makes 8 • Ready in 4 hrs 30 mins

90g (3oz) plain flour
1tsp ground nutmeg
1tsp mixed spice
1tsp cinnamon
90g (3oz) dark muscovado sugar
45g (1½oz) dry white breadcrumbs
100g (3½oz) vegan suet
½tsp baking powder
2tbsp black treacle
6tbsp brandy or rum
Finely grated zest and juice of 1 orange and 1 lemon
2tbsp beetroot powder (from health food shops) or ¼tsp red colouring (optional)
1 apple, peeled and grated
250g (9oz) mixed dried fruit
200g (7oz) dried figs, chopped
5tbsp maple syrup
2tbsp brandy or rum
Edible gold glitter
1 fig, cut into wedges

You will need
6-8 individual pudding basins, greased and the bases lined with baking paper, plus extra baking paper, foil and string

1 Combine the flour, nutmeg, mixed spice, cinnamon, sugar, breadcrumbs, suet and baking powder in a large mixing bowl.
2 Pour the black treacle, brandy, citrus zests and juices, and beetroot powder into the flour mixture.
3 Pile in the grated apple, dried fruit and dried figs. Mix everything together thoroughly with a large spoon. Divide the mixture equally between the pudding basins. Cover each one with baking paper and foil, and secure with string.
4 Cook in a steamer for 4 hrs, topping up the water every 30 mins or as needed.
5 To serve, warm the maple syrup and brandy or rum and sprinkle in edible gold glitter.
6 Upturn the puddings onto plates, top with a fig wedge and drizzle over the warm maple syrup, brandy or rum and edible glitter mixture.

Per serving: Cals 444, Fat 12g, Sat fat 6g, Carbs 71g

Vegan figgy puds

WINTER

Chocolate orange trifle

SOMETHING SWEET

TIP
We used 2 medium-sized hemisphere cake pans from Lakeland but you could use 2 x 15cm (6in) diameter pudding basins instead.

Christmas bombe

SEASONAL COOKBOOK woman&home 145

WINTER

Chocolate orange trifle

Buy easy-peel clementines. For an alcohol-free version, swap the Cointreau for orange juice

Serves 10 • Ready in 25 mins, plus cooling

450ml (15fl oz) full-fat milk
1 vanilla pod, split
3 eggs, plus 2 yolks
50g (2oz) caster sugar
4tsp cornflour
500g (1lb) chocolate chip brioche, sliced 1cm (½in) thick
4tbsp Cointreau or Triple Sec
700g (1lb 8oz) clementines, peeled and soaked in the Cointreau, then sliced into rounds (reserve the Cointreau)
600ml (20fl oz) double cream
4tbsp icing sugar
To decorate
Zest of 1 orange and chocolate curls
You will need
A deep 3l (6pt) trifle bowl

1 Heat the milk and vanilla pod until you see steam coming off the surface. Remove from the heat and set aside. Whisk the eggs, yolks, sugar and cornflour together. Discard the vanilla pod and gradually whisk the milk into the egg mixture.
2 Pour into a clean pan and cook over a gentle heat, stirring, for 5 mins until thicker and smooth. Strain and leave to cool with a layer of clingfilm pressed onto the top to prevent a skin forming.
3 Lay the brioche slices on a plate and drizzle over the Cointreau. Put half the slices in the base of the trifle bowl and scatter over half the clementine rounds before pouring over half the cooled custard.
4 Whip the cream, icing sugar and reserved liqueur until it forms loose peaks; spoon half onto the fruit. Scatter with remaining brioche, fruit and custard, then top with the remaining cream. Sprinkle over the orange zest and chocolate curls. Chill until ready to serve.
Per serving: Cals 641, Fat 43g, Sat fat 25g, Carbs 49g

Christmas bombe

Get ahead for the big day! Make up to step 2 and keep in the freezer until you're ready to decorate

Serves 16 • Ready in 30 mins, plus overnight freezing and chilling

1 pandoro (an Italian cake similar to panettone but without the fruit)
100ml (3½fl oz) Southern Comfort liqueur
600ml (20fl oz) double cream
2tsp caramel flavouring
50g (2oz) golden caster sugar
1tsp vanilla bean paste
100g (3½oz) salted caramel chocolate, chopped
100g (3½oz) shelled unsalted pistachio nuts, chopped
100g (3½oz) stem ginger, chopped
300g (10½oz) raspberries
For the decoration
200g (7oz) dark chocolate
100ml (3½fl oz) double cream
Silver star sprinkle decorations
75g (3oz) white chocolate, broken into squares
Chocolate balls
You will need
2 x 15cm (6in) hemisphere cake pans (or pudding basins), lined with clingfilm, plus holly leaves, to decorate

1 Cut the pandoro cake in half across the centre and scoop out the soft centre (you can save this for eating or use in a trifle). Press the cake shells into each cake pan, pressing it against the sides. Drizzle over the Southern Comfort.
2 Whip together the cream, caramel flavouring, golden caster sugar and vanilla bean paste until it forms soft peaks. Lightly fold in the salted caramel chocolate, pistachios, stem ginger and raspberries. Spoon half the mixture into each of the cake-lined pans, spreading the surface level. Join together to make a bombe. Wrap tightly with clingfilm and freeze overnight.
3 Remove the pans and peel off the clingfilm. Cut a thin slice off the base to stop it rolling, and place on a serving plate.
4 To decorate, place the dark chocolate and double cream in a small pan and heat until melted and smooth. Stir and allow the mixture to cool slightly, then spread over the pudding to cover it completely. Scatter over the silver star decorations and press them lightly into the chocolate. Melt the white chocolate in a bowl over a pan of simmering water and spoon over the top of the pudding. Chill for 30 mins before serving. Decorate with holly and red lustred caramel balls.
Per serving: Cals 636, Fat 44g, Sat fat 25g, Carbs 48g

> **TIP** Filled with a surprise centre of salted caramel, chocolate, pistachio, ginger and raspberry cream, the Christmas bombe is a real showstopper

Raspberry meringue bombe

A prepare-ahead pud that's well worth the forward planning

Serves 8 • Ready in 30 mins, plus freezing

750ml (1pt) vanilla ice cream
250ml (½pt) raspberry sorbet
½ Madeira loaf cake, sliced
4tbsp Bacardi or apple juice
4 egg whites
160g (5½oz) caster sugar
To decorate
Icing sugar, edible glitter and mini edible silver stars
You will need
A 1l (2pt) pudding basin lined with a double layer of clingfilm, plus festive cupcake topper decorations

1 Tip the ice cream into the basin, pressing it up the sides to create a hole in the centre. Scoop the sorbet into the centre of the ice cream.
2 Arrange the cake slices on top, trimming so the sorbet and ice cream are covered completely. Drizzle the Bacardi or apple juice over the cake. Cover with clingfilm and freeze for at least 2 hrs or up to 1 week.
3 On the day of serving, whisk the egg whites until stiff, then whisk in the sugar 1tbsp at a time, until thick and glossy.
4 Turn the frozen pudding out onto a heatproof plate. Quickly spread and swirl the meringue over the pudding to completely cover then pop back in the freezer until you are ready to serve.
5 To serve, heat the oven to 200°C/400°F/Gas 6 and bake the pudding for 4-5 mins until the meringue is golden. Decorate with a dusting of icing sugar, edible glitter, silver stars and Christmas decorations. Serve immediately before it melts.
Per serving: Cals 324, Fat 4g, Sat fat 2g, Carbs 63g

Miso prawn skewers

Our kind of PARTY

Open the bubbly and get the festive season started with these delicious, easy-to-make nibbles

OUR KIND OF PARTY

Miso prawn skewers

Low in calories but high in flavour – finger food at its finest

Makes 12 or 24 • Ready in 20 mins, plus marinating

12 raw tiger prawns or 24 medium-sized prawns, peeled but head and tails left intact
Juice of ½ lemon
3tbsp white miso paste
2tbsp olive oil
Lemon wedges and chopped spring onions or chives, to serve

1 Mix the prawns with the lemon juice and miso paste, and refrigerate for 30 mins, to marinate.
2 Thread each prawn onto a skewer (or two prawns if using smaller ones). Place on a baking tray, drizzle with oil and grill for 3-4 mins each side, or a little less if using smaller prawns, until charred and cooked through. Serve with lemon wedges, and spring onions or chives.
Per serving: Cals 27, Fat 2g, Sat fat 0.3g, Carbs 0.5g

TIP Miso is a fermented soya bean paste with a rich savoury flavour. It's also good for marinating chunks of rump or sirloin steak and chicken breast

SEASONAL COOKBOOK woman&home 149

WINTER

TIP
You can freeze these before baking, then bake from frozen allowing an extra 5-10 mins cooking time.

Asian sausage rolls

150 woman&home SEASONAL COOKBOOK

Asian sausage rolls

A party must-have, with an added spicy zing!

Makes 22 • Ready in 45 mins

400g (14oz) minced pork
3tbsp kecap manis (sweet soy sauce)
1tbsp sesame oil
4 spring onions, finely sliced
¼tsp Chinese five spice
½tsp dried chilli flakes
375g (13½oz) pack puff pastry
1 egg, beaten
2tbsp sesame seeds
Chilli sauce, for dipping

1 Mix the mince with the kecap manis, sesame oil, spring onions, five spice and chilli flakes, and season well.
2 Heat the oven to 200°C/400°F/Gas 6. Roll out the pastry to 30x50cm (12x20in). Cut the pastry in half lengthways. Roll the mince mixture into two long sausages and place one down the centre of each piece of pastry. Brush down one side of each piece of pastry with beaten egg. Fold the pastry over to cover the filling and press with a fork to seal.
3 Brush the pastry with egg and sprinkle with sesame seeds. Cut the long rolls into 3cm (1¼in) pieces and place on a baking tray. Bake for 30 mins until golden. Cool slightly then serve with chilli sauce, for dipping.
Per serving: Cals 108, Fat 7g, Sat fat 3g, Carbs 6g

Smoked salmon filo bites

So simple to make and yet so impressive

Makes 30 • Ready in 20 mins, plus cooling

4 sheets filo pastry
40g (1½oz) butter, melted
1 egg, beaten
Small bunch dill
150g (5oz) pack Boursin cheese
200g (7oz) pack smoked salmon, cut into strips
Lemon wedges, to serve

1 Heat the oven to 180°C/350°F/Gas 4. Lay the filo pastry out on a board. Brush one sheet with melted butter and egg, and scatter over small sprigs of dill. Top with another sheet of filo and repeat. Continue the layering with all the sheets of filo, finishing with a final brush of butter.
2 Cut the pastry into bite-sized triangles and place on a baking tray. Bake for 5-8 mins until golden and crisp. Leave to cool.
3 To serve, spoon a little Boursin on to each pastry bite and top with a ruffle of smoked salmon, a sprig of dill and a grinding of black pepper. Serve with lemon wedges.
Per filo bite: Cals 61, Fat 4g, Sat fat 0.5g, Carbs 1.2g

TIP Top with prawns instead of salmon or for a veggie topping use antipasti artichokes from a jar

Fondue with mini roasties

TIP Chunks of crusty bread are an easy alternative to potatoes, or the cheese fondue is also good served with lightly cooked cauliflower and mushrooms.

Fondue with mini roasties

Crispy roast potatoes dipped in melted cheese – absolute heaven!

Serves 6-8 • Ready in 45 mins

750g (1½lb) baby new potatoes, halved if large
2tbsp olive oil
3 sprigs of thyme
100g (3½oz) Comte cheese, grated
100g (3½oz) Gruyere cheese, grated
100g (3½oz) Emmental cheese, grated
2tsp cornflour
1 garlic clove, halved
350ml (12fl oz) dry white wine
Small glass of Calvados or kirsch

1 Heat the oven to 200°C/400°F/Gas 6. Tip the potatoes into a large roasting tin, drizzle over the oil and toss with the thyme and a pinch of sea salt. Roast for 20-25 mins until cooked and golden.
2 Meanwhile, mix together the cheeses and cornflour. Rub the base of a pan with the garlic, then discard. Add the wine to the pan and heat until simmering gently.
3 Gradually add the cheese, a handful at a time, stirring and melting between each addition. When all the cheese has been added and the mixture has thickened slightly, stir in the Calvados or kirsch. Pour into a bowl, top with a grinding of black pepper, and serve with the potatoes for dipping.
Per serving (to serve 6): Cals 387, Fat 21g, Sat fat 11g, Carbs 21g

Spiced lamb koftas with minty cucumber raita

Fuss-free mini versions of these tasty kebabs

Makes 12 • Ready in 30 mins, plus chilling

500g (1lb) lean minced lamb
1 red onion, finely chopped
2 garlic cloves, crushed
2tsp garam masala
1 small red chilli, chopped
Small bunch mint leaves, chopped
1tbsp sunflower oil
For the raita:
½ small cucumber, coarsely grated
200g (7oz) natural yoghurt
Small bunch mint leaves, finely chopped
½tsp ground cumin
2 spring onions, chopped

1 Mix together the lamb mince, onion, garlic, garam masala, chilli and mint, and season well. Divide the mixture into 12 even portions and form into sausage shapes around wooden skewers. Chill for 30 mins.
2 Heat the oil in a pan, add the skewers in batches and fry over a medium heat for 6-8 mins until browned and cooked through. Keep warm in a low oven.
3 For the raita, squeeze excess liquid from the cucumber then mix with the yoghurt, mint, cumin and spring onions. Season and serve with the koftas.
Per serving: Cals 135, Fat 8.5g, Sat fat 4g, Carbs 2g

TIP You can roast the koftas in the oven instead of frying them. Drizzle with oil and cook at 200°C/400°F/Gas 6 for 20 mins

OUR KIND OF PARTY

Spiced lamb koftas with minty cucumber raita

Tikka prawn poppadom bites
Recipe overleaf

SEASONAL COOKBOOK **woman&home** 153

WINTER

Tikka prawn poppadom bites

Curried prawns, poppadoms and mango chutney all in one tasty mouthful

Serves 8 • Ready in 20 mins

1tbsp tikka curry paste (such as Patak's)
150g (5oz) raw, peeled prawns
1tbsp sunflower oil
2½tbsp mango chutney
2½tbsp Greek yoghurt
16 mini poppadoms
Coriander leaves, to serve

1 Mix together the tikka paste and prawns and leave to marinate for 10 mins. Heat the oil in a frying pan until hot, add the prawns and stir-fry for 1-2 mins until pink and cooked through.
2 Stir the mango chutney and yoghurt together and put a teaspoonful of the mixture on to each poppadom. Top with a prawn and coriander leaf.
Per serving: Cals 40, Fat 2g, Sat fat 0.5g, Carbs 3g

> **TIP** The prawns can be cooked and chilled several hours in advance ready to assemble the poppadoms just before serving

A trio of dips

154 woman&home SEASONAL COOKBOOK

OUR KIND OF PARTY

A trio of dips

Whizz these up ahead of time and serve with a selection of bread, crackers and veg sticks

TAPENADE

Serves 10 • Ready in 5 mins

300g (10½oz) pitted black olives
5 anchovy fillets
1 garlic clove, crushed
30g (1oz) capers
3tbsp extra virgin olive oil

1 Pulse everything in a food processor until you have a coarse, but not too chunky, mixture.
Per serving: Cals 134, Fat 2g, Sat fat 2g, Carbs 6g

BABA GANOUSH

Serves 10 • Ready in 1 hr

3 medium aubergines
4tbsp extra virgin olive oil
2 garlic cloves
2½tbsp tahini
1tsp ground cumin
3tbsp lemon juice (approx 1 lemon)
Handful of fresh parsley, chopped
Pomegranate seeds (optional)

1 Heat the oven to 180°C/350°F/Gas 4. Cut the aubergines in half lengthways, and score the flesh in a criss-cross pattern, being careful not to cut through the skin. Rub the aubergine halves with 2tbsp of the oil, arrange on a baking tray skin side down and bake for around 45 mins until the flesh is soft. Leave to cool.
2 Place the garlic, tahini, cumin, remaining olive oil, aubergine flesh (discard the skins) and lemon juice into a food processor and blitz until smooth and creamy. Season to taste and scatter with parsley and pomegranate seeds, if using.
Per serving: Cals 83, Fat 7g, Sat fat 1g, Carbs 2g

HUMMUS

Serves 20 • Ready in 10 mins

2x400g (14oz) cans chickpeas
2tbsp tahini
2 garlic cloves, crushed
4tbsp lemon juice
5tbsp extra virgin olive oil, plus extra, to drizzle
Smoked paprika

1 Drain the chickpeas and set aside the liquid. Rinse the chickpeas and tip into a food processor.
2 Add the tahini, garlic, lemon juice, a few tablespoons of chickpea water and blitz. Set the speed to slow and gradually pour in the oil. Add more chickpea water, if needed, until you have a smooth dip consistency. Season, dust with smoked paprika and drizzle with olive oil, to serve.
Per serving: Cals 71, Fat 5g, Sat fat 1g, Carbs 4g

TIP These dips will keep in the fridge for two days. Any leftovers are great served in wraps with salad for lunch

TIP Swap the beef mince to Quorn or other meat-free mince alternatives to make this a vegetarian dish.

Mexican meatballs

OUR KIND OF PARTY

Mexican meatballs

Serve with a pile of tortilla chips or mini pittas

Serves 10 • Ready in 1 hr 30 mins

2 small onions, finely chopped
1tsp chilli powder
1kg (2lb) beef mince
1tbsp olive oil
4 garlic cloves, crushed
1tbsp chopped dried ancho chillies or 1tsp sweet smoked paprika
2½tsp coriander seeds, crushed
1¼tsp fennel seeds, crushed
½tsp allspice powder
1 cinnamon stick
300g (10½oz) passata
500ml (1pt) beef stock
Good squeeze of lime juice
Large handful fresh coriander leaves, chopped
Soured cream, guacamole and tortilla chips, to serve

1 Mix half the onion and a pinch of the chilli powder with the mince and season well. Shape into 25 meatballs and leave in the fridge for 20 mins to firm up.
2 Heat the oil in a large pan. Add the meatballs and fry, turning occasionally, until browned. Remove from the pan and set aside. Add the remaining onion to the pan and fry for 3 mins. Add the garlic, spices and remaining chilli powder and fry for 1 min. Add the passata and stock and bring to the boil.
3 Reduce the heat and simmer for 15 mins then add the meatballs, cover and simmer for 20-25 mins. Season and stir in the lime juice and most of the coriander. Spoon over some soured cream and sprinkle with remaining coriander. Serve with extra soured cream, guacamole and tortilla chips.
Per serving: Cals 254, Fat 18g, Sat fat 7g Carbs 3g

Cheese straws

Irresistibly moreish – make plenty as they'll disappear fast

Makes 12 • Ready in 40 mins

125g (4½oz) mixed grated cheese (such as Cheddar, Gruyere and Parmesan)
Pinch of cayenne pepper
375g (13oz) pack ready-rolled puff pastry at room temperature
1tsp Marmite, mustard or anchovy paste

1 Mix the cheeses with cayenne and season well. Unroll the pastry and brush with a little Marmite, mustard or anchovy paste. Sprinkle over most of the cheese and press down lightly. Cut the pastry widthways into 2cm (¾in) strips.
2 Twist each strip, place on a baking tray and sprinkle over the remaining cheese. Chill for 10 mins.
3 Heat the oven to 200°C/400°F/Gas 6. Bake the cheese straws for 10-15 mins until golden and crisp.
Per serving: Cals 159, Fat 11g, Sat fat 6g, Carbs 11g

TIP You can use pesto instead of Marmite, mustard or anchovy paste for a flavour change or sprinkle the twists with poppy seeds or sesame seeds before baking

SEASONAL COOKBOOK woman&home 157

WINTER

MY SWEET VALENTINE

Why not make one of these irresistible bakes for your loved one?

Jammy heart dodgers

Jammy heart dodgers

Pair these cuties with a cuppa

Makes 24 • Ready in 40 mins, plus chilling

For the biscuits:
25g (1oz) butter, softened
60g (2½oz) icing sugar
A few drops of vanilla extract
200g (7oz) plain flour
For the filling:
8-10tbsp strawberry jam
Icing sugar, for dusting
You will need:
A 5cm (2in) round, fluted cutter and a small heart cutter; plus baking trays lined with baking paper

1 Heat the oven to 180°C/350°F/Gas 4. Beat together the butter, icing sugar and vanilla until light and fluffy. Gradually add the flour and mix to form a dough. Wrap in clingfilm and chill for 20 mins.
2 Roll out the dough on a lightly floured surface to about 5mm (¼in) thick, and cut out rounds with the fluted cutter. Cut out hearts from the centre of half of the rounds, then re-roll the trimmings to make more biscuits.
3 Place the biscuits on the lined trays and bake for 12-15 mins. Remove from the oven then transfer to a wire rack to cool.
4 Sandwich the biscuits using jam, and dust with icing sugar. The sugar will dissolve to give shiny red centres.
Per biscuit: Cals 62, Fat 1g, Sat fat 0.5g, Carbs 12g

MY SWEET VALENTINE

Berry tart

This tastes as good as it looks!

Easy/Prepare ahead
- Serves 10 • Ready in 1 hr, plus cooling and chilling

200g (7oz) plain flour
75g (3oz) ground almonds
40g (1½oz) icing sugar
100g (3½oz) butter
A few drops of almond extract
3 eggs, plus 4 egg yolks, all beaten
Zest of 2 lemons
300ml (10fl oz) whipping cream
1½tbsp cornflour mixed with 2tbsp milk
50g (2oz) caster sugar
500g (½lb) mixed redcurrants, raspberries and small strawberries, quartered
100g (3½oz) seedless strawberry conserve, sieved
White chocolate hearts

You will need
A 23cm (9in) fluted tart tin, baking paper and baking beans

1 Put the flour, almonds, sugar, butter and almond extract in a processor and pulse until it forms breadcrumbs. Add 1 egg, 1tbsp at a time, and pulse until it forms a dough. Chill for 15 mins. Heat the oven to 190°C/375°F/Gas 5.
2 Roll out the dough to the thickness of a £1 coin, and press it into the tin, trimming any excess. Prick with a fork, fill with baking paper then beans, and bake blind for 20 mins. Remove the beans and baking paper and cook for a further 10 mins until golden. Reduce the oven to 180°C/350°F/Gas 4.
3 Whisk the remaining eggs and yolks, lemon zest, cream, cornflour and caster sugar in a pan, put on a low heat and stir until thickened, about 5 mins. Strain through a sieve into a jug. Fill the tart case with the mix, then bake for 20-25 mins until just set. Leave to cool; chill for 2 hrs.
4 Mix the berries with jam and add to the tart. Decorate with hearts.
Per serving: Cals 480, Fat 31g, Sat fat 15g, Carbs 39g

Berry tart

WINTER

Perfect PANCAKES

Celebrate in style on Pancake Day – although these recipes are flipping great at any time!

Multigrain pancakes with poached rhubarb

Light, fluffy and full of flavour! Stack them high and get stuck in

Serves 6 (Makes 18) • Ready in 30 mins

For the pancakes:
100g (3½oz) oat flour
75g (3oz) buckwheat flour
2tsp baking powder
¾tsp bicarbonate of soda
75g (3oz) granulated sugar
45g (1½oz) rolled oats
350ml (12fl oz) buttermilk
300ml (10oz) oat milk
1 egg
50g (2oz) unsalted butter, melted
Handful of pomegranate seeds, to serve

For the poached rhubarb:
400g (14oz) rhubarb, trimmed and cut into 5cm (2in) pieces
300ml (10oz) pomegranate juice
1 vanilla pod
1 orange, zest pared with a vegetable peeler
150g (5oz) caster sugar
2 star anise

Multigrain pancakes with poached rhubarb

1 In a large bowl, sift the flours, baking powder, bicarb, sugar and ¾tsp salt, and stir through the oats. In a jug, whisk the buttermilk, oat milk and the egg. Add to the dry ingredients and whisk until smooth. Fold through the melted butter and leave to rest.
2 For the poached rhubarb, add the ingredients to a pan and bring to the boil. Turn down the heat, cover and simmer for 5-6 mins, until the rhubarb is just tender. Remove with a slotted spoon and transfer to a dish. Bring the leftover juice to the boil and reduce by two-thirds until thick and syrupy. Strain rhubarb, reserving the syrup.
3 Heat a non-stick frying pan over a medium heat and ladle in the batter. Fry for 3-4 mins until bubbles come to the surface and pop. Flip the pancakes and fry for 2-3 mins on the other side until cooked through. Transfer to a plate and continue to cook the batter to make 18 pancakes.
4 To serve, stack the pancakes, top with the rhubarb, drizzle over the syrup and scatter with the pomegranate seeds.
Per serving: Cals 503, Fat 12g, Sat fat 6g, Carbs 86g

Ice-cream sundae crepe

Combine two winning treats in one with this folded crepe

Serves 4 • Ready in 30 mins

For the pancakes:
100g (3½oz) plain flour
2 eggs
300ml (10oz) milk
Butter, for frying
For the filling:
500ml (17fl oz) raspberry ripple ice cream
200g (7oz) frozen mixed berries, defrosted
4tbsp pecans broken up, for sprinkling
8tbsp maple syrup

1 Put the flour in a bowl, add the eggs and milk and whisk to make a smooth batter with the consistency of double cream.
2 Heat a little butter in a 15cm (6in) non-stick frying pan. Pour in just enough

160 woman&home SEASONAL COOKBOOK

PERFECT PANCAKES

Ice-cream sundae crepe

Tiramisu crepe cake

mixture to cover the base of the pan, tilt to cover and cook for around 30 seconds until the base has set. Use a palette knife to flip over the pancake and cook for a further few seconds until golden. Repeat with the remaining batter mixture.
3 Place a couple of scoops of ice cream on to each pancake, then spoon over berries. Fold over pancake, sprinkle with pecans and drizzle with maple syrup.
Per serving: Cals 692, Fat 42g, Sat fat 15g, Carbs 68g

Tiramisu crepe cake

This stunning layered cake is a fun alternative for a special occasion – it looks impressive and anyone can do it

Serves 16 • Ready in 1 hr

For the crepes:
250g (9oz) plain flour
4 eggs
450ml (15fl oz) whole milk
2tbsp espresso powder
15g (1tbsp) butter
For the filling:
600g (21oz) whipping cream
500g (17½oz) mascarpone
1tbsp espresso powder
75ml (2½ fl oz) Marsala wine
Cocoa powder

1 For the crepes, whisk the flour, eggs, milk, espresso powder and a pinch of salt in a bowl. Melt the butter in a 25cm (9½in) crepe pan or frying pan. Ladle the batter, swirling the pan to leave a thin coating. Repeat to make 24 crepes.
2 For the filling, place the cream and mascarpone in a bowl and whisk to form soft peaks. Remove a third of the mixture and add the espresso powder to this third. Whisk gently to medium peaks and set aside in the fridge. Add the Marsala to the remaining cream and whisk through to medium peaks.
3 To assemble, place a crepe on to a serving plate or cake stand and add 2-3tbsp of cream, spreading to the edges with a small palette knife or spoon. Top with another crepe and repeat until you have used all the cream and crepes. Add the coffee cream to a piping bag fitted with a round nozzle and pipe small bulbs all over the surface of the cake.
Dust with cocoa powder and serve.
Per serving: Cals 390, Fat 32g, Sat fat 20g, Carbs 16g

TIP These pancakes freeze really well. Place greaseproof paper between each pancake and put in a food bag. Defrost by placing in a toaster

SEASONAL COOKBOOK **woman&home**

woman&home
SEASONAL COOKBOOK

Future PLC Quay House, The Ambury, Bath, BA1 1UA

Bookazine Editorial
Editor **Zara Gaspar**
Designer **Briony Duguid**
Compiled by **Philippa Grafton & Madelene King**
Head of Art & Design **Greg Whitaker**
Editorial Director **Jon White**
Managing Director **Grainne McKenna**

woman&home Editorial
Group Editor **Hannah Fernando**
Group Creative Director **Phil Attaway**
Lifestyle Content Director **Charlotte Richards**
Group Food Director **Jen Bedloe**

Photography
All copyrights and trademarks are recognised and respected

Advertising
Media packs are available on request
Commercial Director **Clare Dove**

International
Head of Print Licensing **Rachel Shaw**
licensing@futurenet.com
www.futurecontenthub.com

Circulation
Head of Newstrade **Tim Mathers**

Production
Head of Production **Mark Constance**
Production Project Manager **Matthew Eglinton**
Advertising Production Manager **Joanne Crosby**
Digital Editions Controller **Jason Hudson**
Production Managers **Keely Miller, Nola Cokely, Vivienne Calvert, Fran Twentyman**

Printed in the UK

Distributed by Marketforce, www.marketforce.co.uk – For enquiries, please email: mfcommunications@futurenet.com

woman&home Seasonal Cookbook Second Edition (LBZ5958)
© 2024 Future Publishing Limited

All content previously appeared in this edition of
woman&home Seasonal Cookbook First Edition

We are committed to only using magazine paper which is derived from responsibly managed, certified forestry and chlorine-free manufacture. The paper in this bookazine was sourced and produced from sustainable managed forests, conforming to strict environmental and socioeconomic standards.

All contents © 2024 Future Publishing Limited or published under licence. All rights reserved. No part of this magazine may be used, stored, transmitted or reproduced in any way without the prior written permission of the publisher. Future Publishing Limited (company number 2008885) is registered in England and Wales. Registered office: Quay House, The Ambury, Bath BA1 1UA. All information contained in this publication is for information only and is, as far as we are aware, correct at the time of going to press. Future cannot accept any responsibility for errors or inaccuracies in such information. You are advised to contact manufacturers and retailers directly with regard to the price of products/services referred to in this publication. Apps and websites mentioned in this publication are not under our control. We are not responsible for their contents or any other changes or updates to them. This magazine is fully independent and not affiliated in any way with the companies mentioned herein.

FUTURE Connectors. Creators. Experience Makers.

Future plc is a public company quoted on the London Stock Exchange (symbol: FUTR)
www.futureplc.com

Chief Executive **Jon Steinberg**
Non-Executive Chairman **Richard Huntingford**
Chief Financial and Strategy Officer **Penny Ladkin-Brand**

Tel +44 (0)1225 442 244